THE

> *When the Thirsty Are Led by the Delirious*

LEADERSHIP DROUGHT

CORTES "JODY" BICKING, PhD,
and KEVIN B. McKENZIE

THE LEADERSHIP DROUGHT
When the Thirsty Are Led by the Delirious

iUniverse books may be ordered through booksellers or by contacting:

iUniverse
1663 Liberty Drive
Bloomington, IN 47403
www.iuniverse.com
1-800-Authors (1-800-288-4677)

All Scriptures are taken from the Holy Bible, King James Version (Authorized Version). First published in 1611. Quoted from the KJV Classic Reference Bible, Copyright © 1983 by The Zondervan Corporation.

ISBN: 978-1-5320-2795-6 (sc)
ISBN: 978-1-5320-2796-3 (hc)
ISBN: 978-1-5320-2797-0 (e)

Library of Congress Control Number: 2017913029

Print information available on the last page.

iUniverse rev. date: 11/21/2017

CONTENTS

PREFACE

"We won, didn't we?" These words, spoken by Senator Harry Reid, define the leadership character of our time. The ends justify the means—any means.

There is no argument that such a philosophy has been used throughout history. It has been used as justification for some horrifying actions that a few believed necessary, given the particular situation. But when such a philosophy becomes justification for mainstream daily practice, the time has come for serious reflection. The time has come to review and consider the foundational principles of our leadership practice. We must ask what has become of a proud leadership history that enabled us to evolve as the greatest country in history, even with our warts. The day Senator Reid stated, "We won, didn't we!" *The Leadership Drought* was proclaimed!

Experiencing Drought Conditions

As partners in ACHEV, Kevin and Jody have participated in many projects, but two are significant and deserve particular mention with regard to the concepts expressed in this book.

The first was a project commissioned by a $2 billion per year, privately owned, international, industrial-processing and distribution company. ACHEV was charged with providing consulting and training services aimed at reversing some alarming trends developing in the company's ongoing employee engagement survey. The list of low-ranked areas of concern included the following:

- employee recognition
- protecting individual "turf"
- clear lines of communication

- promotion of people with potential to be high performers
- honest and open internal dialogue
- open sharing of information
- attracting and hiring talented employees
- willingness to embrace change
- praise for employees who improve the quality of products and services
- spirit of cooperation among all organizational levels

The senior leaders tended to believe their situation was unique, as compared to other industries and organizations. However, a cursory review of organizational development and leadership literature indicated this list accurately described many organizations at that time—and still would do so today.

ACHEV partners and employees undertook three months of interviews, investigation, and research before presenting recommendations for possible courses of action. We determined that the main focus of effort should be on the leadership. ACHEV's leadership engagement and alignment process (LEAP) was born.

Our relationship with the company continued for eleven years before budget and significant internal changes brought the project to a close. The last employee engagement survey indicated significant improvement in the following indicators (these surveys were all administered and controlled by an outside, unaffiliated industrial psychology firm):

- Forty-nine of fifty-one items improved.
- Average item scores rose 54 percent.
- Ninety-four percent of the survey items scored above the target average.

During the course of the project, we delivered a two-and-a-half-day program from two to four times each year. After each program, the company surveyed participants. Based upon the feedback received, incremental changes were made at the conclusion of each session. At the end of the last program, participants assigned scores that averaged 76 percent "exceeded my expectations," which was 2 percent higher than the cumulative average rating for the sixty-plus presentations spanning the previous eleven years.

Through referrals, ACHEV delivered similar programs to firms in the metals distribution, hospital construction, software development, financial services, credit union, medical services, and community banking industries.

* * *

Our second significant project involved a company that developed and distributed a customer relationship management (CRM) software program for the community banking industry. Initially, ACHEV was engaged to deliver leadership development programs and executive coaching. At the conclusion of one such meeting, the CEO mentioned the existence of a marketing issue that was becoming a serious concern.

The software business model was built upon two sources of revenue: first, the initial fee; second, and most importantly, the periodic renewal and update fee. The problem was obvious. Interestingly, 50 percent of the client banks literally loved and were adamant supporters of our client's product and services. The other 50 percent (the numbers in fact broke fifty-fifty) paid the initial fee, went through the installation and training process, and then did not renew and rarely used the ancillary systems available—a true barbell analogy. The firm had tried annual conventions, surveys, and direct questioning; the problem remained unresolved.

ACHEV was engaged to make planned, announced visits to a selection of banks in an effort to determine the reasons behind the differentiation. We made visits over several months to representative banks from Vermont to California. After a visit to a client bank in Manhattan, Kansas, we experienced an epiphany.

During our visit, first thing in the morning, a meeting of the senior officers was convened. The president and CEO, though an early riser, announced he was busy and did not feel it necessary to attend the kickoff meeting. His competent and hand-picked assistant vice president of information services (who was also the CEO's son-in-law) could "handle matters of this magnitude."

This incident triggered further research on our part to determine the level of active participation among all client banks' senior leadership. Banks whose top leader actively engaged (signed in) with the system daily were always the banks who loved the product. The banks whose top leader did not engage dominated the nonrenewal list.

ACHEV designed and delivered a presentation entitled "Successful Connections." It was a half-day workshop for board members and senior officers, constructed to show the bank leadership how to use their corporate vision—usually some statement about concern for people and customer service—to assimilate the Connections product into their banks. The presentation also showed leadership how to employ that vision statement in their hiring and feedback processes.

We delivered this program to sixty-three community banks across the country. What became apparent was that most of these businesses had little or no familiarity with their own vision statements, let alone any comprehension of the utility these statements offered leaders. For a couple of years, ACHEV stayed very busy delivering vision development retreats for community banks. A few creative bankers also used ACHEV as a business development tool for their commercial customers.

We learned a great many leadership lessons while delivering the vision presentations. While it was increasingly obvious to us that a leadership competency gap existed, it took the financial crisis of 2008 to make it apparent to the many, whether stockholders or employees, that the success their companies had enjoyed was not the result of leadership, but in spite of it.

Leadership as a Calling and Significant Personal Responsibility

Kevin and Jody share a passion for leadership for several reasons. First, they were raised to respect leaders and to understand the awesome responsibility leadership entails. Leadership is a 24-7 job, regardless of the level. Decisions leaders make impact not only the immediate situation, but also the lives of families for years to come. That impact can be good or bad. For the most part, a leader rarely knows the ultimate impact of what may seem like a "routine" decision.

Through their lives and leadership experiences, Kevin and Jody have come to believe that most leadership problems filter down into a handful of ongoing issues. Regardless of the seeming complexity of the problems faced, great leaders have the ability to look past the symptoms and find pathways to solutions. They understand the value of diversity of experience and perspective, resulting in mutual respect between leaders and those being led. Great leaders recognize that communication and effective collaboration are essential skills, and they know how to develop those skills in others. Great leaders do not presume to have all the answers. They do know how to encourage and facilitate the best thinking in others. Having confidence in their ability to facilitate reflective and creative thinking, they surround themselves with people more talented than themselves, and holding a variety of perspectives and experiences. Surrounded by such diverse people, they employ well-developed listening skills and give recognition and reward for the solutions they hear. Armed with those solutions, they act swiftly, with courage and confidence in their team. Finally, leaders are fully accountable and willing to accept responsibility without blame.

This list of characteristics and skills is not long or very complicated. Yet we are besieged daily with example after example, in business and in government, in which these basic skills seem to be overlooked or not understood. Unfortunately, this is not a recent phenomenon. It has gone on far too long. It is time we recognize the leadership drought.

INTRODUCTION

What constitutes a drought? Drought conditions exist when there is a lack, deficiency, or scarcity. The term *drought* most often refers to a shortage of water. People initially sense the problem from a prolonged inability to quench their thirst. They want water, they need water, and they begin to feel the physical effects of not having water. When human beings are denied water, they suffer delirium. *Delirium* describes an acutely confused state characterized by disorientation, frenzy, and lack of clarity. Science does not provide an exact time period that a human being can survive without water, but scientists generally agree that one week probably marks the limit.

When the substance lacking is not water but leadership, the process of problem recognition, or proclamation of drought conditions, becomes more difficult. The time involved for recognition goes well beyond a week, to months or possibly even years. As we propose in this book, the period could be two to three leadership generations. What is past is not the important consideration. What is of prime consideration is making the recognition that drought conditions in the area of leadership do, in fact, exist.

Drought Conditions Exposed

In 1994, Ronald Heifetz, then director of the Leadership Education Project at the Kennedy School of Government, Harvard University, published *Leadership Without Easy Answers.* He wrote, "Today we face a crisis in leadership in many areas of public and private life." He continued, "In a crisis we tend to look for the wrong kind of leadership. We call for someone with answers, decisions, strength, and a map of the future." He concluded the passage, "We should be calling for leadership that will challenge us to face problems for which there are no simple, painless solutions – problems that require us to learn new ways."[1]

Ram Charan published *Leaders at All Levels* in 2008. The book's first paragraph states, "Crisis may be an overused word, but it's a fair description of the state of leadership in today's corporations."[2]

David Marquet published *Turn the Ship Around* in 2012. The book is a true "worst to first" account of Captain Marquet's experience as the commander of a US Navy nuclear submarine. In the introduction, he states:

> People are frustrated. Most of us are ready to give it our all when we start a job. We are usually full of ideas for ways to do things better. We eagerly offer our whole intellectual capacity only to be told that is not our job, that it's been tried before, or that we shouldn't rock the boat. Initiative is viewed with skepticism. Our suggestions are ignored. We are told to follow instructions. Our work is reduced to following a set of prescriptions…. With resignation, we get by. Too often, that's where the story of our work life ends.[3]

In 2016, James Kouzes, Dean's Executive Fellow of Leadership at the Leavey School of Business, Santa Clara University, and Barry Posner, an endowed professor at the same institution, wrote:

> There is a leadership shortage in the world. It is not a shortage of potential talent. The people are out there. The eagerness is out there. The resources are out there. The capability is out there. The shortage is a result of three primary factors: demographic shifts, insufficient training and experiences, and prevailing mindsets that discourage people from learning to lead.[4]

The Thirsty and the Delirious

For more than twenty years, recognized leadership authorities have been warning about the lack of real leadership in government and corporate America. Charan, Kouzes, and Posner all agree there is no shortage of raw talent. According to these leading authorities, the lack of know-how in developing talent is the major problem. Barbara Kellerman, the James McGregor Burns Professor in Public Leadership at Harvard, openly admits she is increasingly uneasy about leadership in the twenty-first century and the gap between the teaching of leadership and the practice of leadership.[5]

We hope the title of this book is catchy enough to gain attention across the broad spectrum of possible readers who are touched every day by the actions of leaders in business and government. We also hope that, while catchy, the title sheds a bright light on the low level of skill demonstrated by these leaders. Since you have read this far, we hope you realize the title conveys more than sarcasm; it tells the truth concerning the level of leadership we have now come to accept.

Is there a drought? We believe there is no need to look further than the comments of Heifetz, Charan, Marquet, Kouzes, Posner, and Kellerman. Are there people who have a real thirst for true leadership but are forced to follow "leaders" who are disoriented and frenzied and offer little or no clarity? We believe that the act of watching the daily news offers all the proof necessary to confirm that many of today's "leaders" in corporate America and government are delirious. In fact, they are posing as the role models that those who thirst for real leadership will be forced to emulate.

If this hypothesis is even remotely true, the future of organizations that have traditionally provided the foundation for growth and success in our country and the world has become much darker.

Who Should Read This Book?

This book is not intended for the successful CEO or senior executive who has already learned everything there is to know about leadership and is quite sated with "success." This book will benefit leaders who have tried and toiled under the example of those who already know everything.

The Leadership Drought provides six core principles that are applicable in any situation. These principles represent the sequence of actions that will set any person who truly thirsts for the right leadership skills on the right path and will keep him or her on the cutting edge for years to come.

How Should This Book Be Read?

Start at the beginning. Preview each chapter carefully to ascertain the level of applicable knowledge you now have concerning the topic. When we say *applicable*, we mean the depth of knowledge that will enable the reader to apply and infuse the message into the team or organization.

After previewing the chapter, read it critically; continually ask yourself what its value is and how it can be applied in your organization. At the end of each chapter, there is a section titled "Exercises for Review and Learning." Take the time to contemplate how the questions could be used to facilitate learning within your team or organization.

We do not recommend skimming or cherry-picking concepts. The chapters are designed to build upon each other in the sequence offered. Our experience, along with a great deal of research, indicates that cherry-picking a principle and trying to implement it without the support of the material offered before and after will result in less than desirable results. The principles we offer have been proven to work when they are used in concert. Success will be found through the application of a holistic mind-set. As Professor Carol Dweck states in her book, *Mindset,* changing people's mind-sets and beliefs—even in the simplest way—can have profound effects.[6]

SECTION 1

People in leadership positions must constantly assess the current situation. They do this by cycling through a series of simple questions to develop current awareness and a sense of future options.

- Where are we now?
- What is good about our current position?
- What potential dangers lie ahead?
- How did we get in this position?
- Where do we need to be?
- How will we get there?

Section 1 of *The Leadership Drought* contains two chapters. Chapter 1 describes the evolution of thoughts and actions that locate the overall state of leadership and organizational development at the beginning of the twenty-first century. We intend to expose the reader to factual history and perspective on how our social and industrial systems have brought us to the collective mind-set of current leadership practice.

Chapter 2 provides an overview of twenty-first-century organizations from a systems perspective. Today's organizations are complex, meaning they comprise many interdependent subunits with varying degrees of autonomy. Each unit and subunit is in a continual state of change. Predictability becomes increasingly difficult. The leadership challenge is an ongoing balancing act between control and emerging innovation. Einstein asserted that we cannot solve current problems by using the same kind of thinking that created them.

Section 1 of *The Leadership Drought* identifies the crying need for change from the old, mechanistic style of thinking to a more collaborative form of systems thinking. At the end of this section, the reader will have gained a level of sensitivity to and understanding of the need for change, and the direction in which such change will proceed.

1

THE EVOLUTION OF THE LEADERSHIP DROUGHT

The skills that got you here are not sufficient to get you there!
–Marshall Goldsmith

How did we get from a society that believed in and respected the nobility of leadership to the present-day cynicism? There are explainable reasons for this change in mind-set. For everyone who is a leader, or aspiring to become one, it is important to consider the validity of the argument. That validity can only be assessed through a grasp of the history that paved the pathway to our current situation. This chapter provides an overview of four stages of incremental change that evolved into current leadership practice.

The Four Stages of Incremental Change

There are four distinct stages that comprise incremental changes in our leadership mind-set, more succinctly described as an evolution. First came the rise of Frederick W. Taylor and his ideas concerning scientific management. Second was the rise in popularity of MBA programs during the 1980s. Third, and concurrent with the elitist mind-set associated with the rise in MBA programs, was what Malcolm Gladwell's exposé in the *New Yorker* described as corporate America's obsession with the "talent mindset."[1]

The fourth stage arises as organizations begin to recognize their social structures as complex adaptive systems (CAS). The recognition of this evolutionary stage remains in its infancy today, still struggling to find identity in the practical world of business and politics.

The focal point of understanding about CAS is in the interaction of the many different agents (people and other entities) that comprise a business or service, and how those agents can more effectively collaborate. The theory is not new, but the current interest developed in the writing and collaboration of a small group of organizational development thought leaders. This group connected the current concept of organization with earlier theories of CAS and leadership, suggesting that our old paradigms and fundamental beliefs no longer serve the bigger picture with respect to maximizing organizational performance.

Frederick Winslow Taylor, "The Father of Scientific Management"

Taylor, who received his mechanical engineering degree by correspondence, spent the majority of his professional life seeking to improve industrial efficiency. He became highly influential in the early nineteen hundreds through his application of engineering principles to work done on the shop floor. His most famous work, *The Principles of Scientific Management*, was published in 1911.

While working as a floor supervisor at Midvale Steel, he noticed that workers did not tend to work themselves or their machines to full capacity, resulting in increased per-unit labor costs. He conducted a quasi-scientific study of men carrying pig iron, for the purpose of determining most efficient load per trip standards, maximum work hours, and the type of man best suited for such work.[2] His star performer was a man named Schmidt, for whom the study was later named. Schmidt was a large European immigrant with little other work experience.

About this study and other findings, Taylor testified to Congress, "I can say without the slightest hesitation, that the science of handling pig-iron is so great that the man who is physically capable of handling pig-iron and is sufficiently phlegmatic and stupid to choose this for an occupation is rarely capable of understanding the science of handling pig-iron."[3]

In fairness, it must be said that Taylor's theories, often called "Taylorism," did lift the productivity of the nation's manufacturing industries well above all previous competitive levels.[4] This was accomplished through four maxims:

- enforced standardization
- enforced adoption
- enforced cooperation
- workers are incapable of understanding what they are doing and need to be told what to do and how to do it by management supervisors

Taylor proclaimed at every opportunity that management must always be in control and that communication was most efficient when done in a top-down manner.[5]

Taylor created several myths concerning his ideas. After revision of his Schmidt study data, at least three times, he boasted that no "Taylorized" firm had ever gone on strike, that companies and workers would experience shorter work hours due to increased efficiency, and that unions would no longer have anything to do. Interestingly, not one of his boasts ever came to fruition.[6] He firmly believed that every work situation has "one best way," and once that was discovered, it deserved maximum enforcement.[7]

Henry Ford is famously quoted as saying, "Why is it every time I ask for a pair of hands, they come with a brain attached?"[8] Arguably the greatest industrialist of the time, Ford paid homage to Taylor. Harvard, one of the first schools to offer a business degree, based its original curriculum on Taylor's principles. James O. McKinsey, founder of McKinsey & Co. and then a professor of accounting at the University of Chicago, became a strong advocate of budgets, accountability, and performance measurement.

There is no argument that Harvard has since grown and improved its business programs. Corporations obviously find value working with McKinsey & Co., as they continue to pay millions of dollars per year for their advice. The point is that strong remnants of Taylor's concepts and teachings still impact the thinking of leaders today, despite the fact that many of his theories have been shown to be little more than fairy tales. He deserves credit for making production more efficient in its early days, but he remains a classic example of "what got you here will not get you there."

The Popularity of MBA Programs

Business degrees achieved a high level of prestige in the early 1980s, but just a decade later that prestige began to erode due to a perceived lack of effectiveness. The lack of effectiveness centered around three recurring criticisms. First, there appears to be too much focus on technical skills, to the exclusion of communication skills. Second, leadership does not seem to be taught with any depth. Creativity and an understanding of entrepreneurship are not apparent in graduates. Third, there is little emphasis on the importance of teamwork as it relates to leadership and overall competitiveness.[9]

In other words, at least a decade of "trained" leaders, now holding or moving into senior positions, may be lacking critical skills and knowledge.

Dr. Richard Boyatzis, a noted leadership author, wrote, "The lack of impact on interpersonal and leadership abilities has been consistently cited as criticisms of MBA programs."[10]

Probably the greatest indictment of our past leadership development achievement comes from Dr. Barbara Kellerman. She proclaims uneasiness about our leadership in the twenty-first century—specifically, the gap between teaching and practice. She places the blame on the "leadership industry": "While the industry has been thriving, growing and prospering beyond anyone's early imagination – leaders are, by and large, performing poorly."[11]

The choice to pursue leadership has become more about the pathway to success, wealth, and power rather than a calling. Too many people now choose leadership as a goal for the purpose of control, of their own future and those of others. Yet the truly effective leaders have learned that leadership is more about giving away control rather than seizing it.

The Talent Myth

Malcolm Gladwell proclaimed that the "talent mindset," one of the outcomes of the MBA phenomenon, had become the new orthodoxy of American management.[12] This unquenchable thirst for talent was the blueprint for the Enron culture and, according to Dr. Carol Dweck, sowed the seeds for its demise.[13] Dweck, a well-regarded researcher in social and developmental psychology, holds a professorship at Stanford University and has written and consulted extensively about what she describes as the "fixed mindset" and the "growth mindset."

Dr. Dweck's extensive research indicates that cultures tending toward the worship of talent force employees to look and act extraordinarily talented. When employees don't deliver at the prescribed level, their personal survival is threatened, causing them to respond with defensiveness, blame, and even dishonesty. They will not admit mistakes or take remedial action.

Further, Dweck's research indicates organizations that tend to thrive are filled with leaders who are not constantly striving to prove they are better than others. They don't stand on a particular pecking order. They constantly ask questions, admit when they don't have the answers, and readily accept their own mistakes. Such a mind-set, the *growth mind-set*, focuses on continuous improvement of the whole through the individual.[14]

Lest there be any misunderstanding—recruiting, hiring, and developing the most talented people will always create advantage, provided they possess the right mind-set. The essence of the talent myth is found in the focus and spirit of the team members. The priority of successful teams is always on the collective achievement of the team and not on individual recognition.

Organizations that exemplify the negative result of the talent mind-set are comprised of people who are obsessed with their own reputations and gain. An organization whose people obsess about the performance of the team and its continuous improvement are the antithesis of the talent mind-set culture. In the long term, the team-oriented organization will always prevail.

Organizations as Complex Adaptive Systems: Control vs. Emergence

Taylorism, or mechanistic thought, treats people and organizations as machines. When the agents (whether mechanisms, individuals, or teams) are stimulated, either by an order or by the press of a button, there is a specific, predetermined reaction. In a machine, assuming proper functionality, the outcome can be predicted with great certainty.

A machine with many moving parts and sets of subsystems is complicated. Complicated systems can be controlled and are predictable. That predictability and the ability to control interactions become far less reliable when people and multiple communication channels become part of the productivity equation. The act of creating, manufacturing, marketing, selling, and servicing a product—the phenomenon we call *business*—creates complexity. The possible number of variations, due to the actions of people, becomes infinite.

How we, as individuals or groups, react to the multitude of possibilities must be a major leadership consideration. There is a vast difference between being complicated and being complex. Leadership can influence outcomes, but we can never completely control them, nor should we want to. It is those unknown and unexpected occurrences that are the genesis of all creativity, innovation, and improvement. The concept of continuous improvement, as competitive advantage, hinges upon the emergence of ideas and options created through complexity.

Yes, there is definite need for management control as a means of measuring the success of organizational direction. But if all we do is build a "machine" that repeats the same actions, discouraging variation in ideas, nothing new or better can emerge. Regardless of the times or the level of technological sophistication, leadership will always be about balancing control and emergence.

A supply chain is actually a complex and dynamic supply and demand network. A supply chain is a system of organizations, people, activities, information, and resources involved in moving a product or service from supplier to customer. Regardless of the industry, that network has a direct impact on the bottom line and competitiveness of the business. Indeed, in today's environment, the best supply chain wins!

When Drs. Choi, Dooley, and Rungtusanatham published their 2001 article, "Supply Networks and Complex Adaptive Systems: Control versus Emergence," in the *Journal of Operations Management*, they created the potential for the next great evolution in productivity. They disclosed to the world that positive outcomes and improvement emerge from within the system rather than from purposeful design by a singular entity.[15] It doesn't matter how big or small the system. But the system does require leadership that nurtures an environment of continuous improvement through collaboration.

The Drought?

After reading about the evolution of leadership thought and adding in all the advances in communication technology, some might ask, where is the drought?

The drought exists because there are at least three generations of "trained" leaders in the workforce currently. Many remain stuck in the mechanistic mind-set of Winslow. That is how they were raised, and it has worked for them. In general, they quietly (sometimes not so quietly) believe, "If it ain't broke, don't fix it."

Newer leaders read, talk to friends, go to training, and return to the workplace excited about a new idea, only to be told it won't work or it's already been done. It is often very difficult to get new ideas heard, let alone tried. Old habits go unchecked from one generation to the next and then become the engrained "way things are done." When the flow of new thinking is shut off or curtailed, the thirst for innovation eventually kills the organization.

Exercises for Reflection and Learning

1. Set up discussion groups (10–12 people) among the leadership team of your organization. Without any coercion or direction, ask them to consider the predominant style of the processes and thinking within the various operations. Do those processes and underlying thinking represent "mechanistic" thinking (control), or do they encourage the diverse capabilities of continuous improvement (emergence)?

2. Arrange an executive (senior leadership) retreat and explore the organizational balance between control and emergence. Be sure to make use of the feedback received from the discussion groups. If the need for change becomes apparent, be sure to include a broad cross-section of employees (senior leaders, leaders, frontline team members) to explore, devise, and implement changes. (See appendix A, "Vroom–Yetton Model.")

2

UNDERSTANDING AND EXERCISING LEADERSHIP IN A COMPLEX ADAPTIVE SYSTEM

There is no security in leadership, only opportunity.
–General Douglas MacArthur

Chapter 1 touched on mechanistic theory and its impact on leadership thinking since the publishing of Taylor's 1911 book, *Scientific Management*. Taylor understood that machines are complicated and, when operating within tolerance, highly predictable. When a machine is working properly, the flipping of a certain switch will produce a predictable result. His utopia was the creation of such a condition across organizational processes, ensuring productivity would dramatically increase. However, a fundamental flaw exists in Taylor's theory—people are not fully predictable.

As Henry Ford found with dismay, a person's actions and attitudes vary from day to day, depending upon a good night's sleep, a fight with a spouse, worry about money, illness, a child's last report card ... the list could go on forever. An employee's depth of understanding about the work he or she is expected to do and its connection to the overall success of the company can also have a significant effect on the level of engagement and enthusiasm the employee displays. In short, people add complexity to every organizational setting.

As the number of people involved in an operation increases, so too does the level of complexity. Complexity adds to the variability of performance outcomes for individual processes and the system as a whole. When leadership thinking and actions move from seeing people as passive units of production (mechanistic fundamental) to highly valued resources of knowledge and experience operating in complex environments, quantum

8

leaps in engagement and productivity become possible. Leadership can then create opportunity through inspired change.

Drucker's Admonition

In 1998, Peter Drucker, the renowned business sage, wrote that much of what was being taught in business schools was either totally wrong or seriously out-of-date. Most of our assumptions about business, technology, and organization are at least fifty years old and have outlived their time.[1]

The period of time referenced by Drucker encompasses many of today's top leaders and a generation to come. The command-and-control leadership methods that successfully guided us to victory in World War II were strongly embraced in the 1950s and 1960s. That style is highly mechanistic, meaning that the leader issues instructions (pushes a button), and the follower responds in a predetermined and exact manner. Such a method is also described as *top-down*. People are simply cogs in the machine, replaceable and interchangeable.

Leadership Theories that Have Mechanistic Foundations

Leadership theories such as "the great man" and trait theories were followed by the concept of charismatic leadership. The underlying idea behind these concepts was that leaders were born, not made. Only certain personalities and behavioral characteristics were deemed to be the stuff from which leaders were made.

Those same arguments can still be heard in major corporations today. While the mechanistic style is not as prominent as it was at the beginning of the 1970s, it continues to hold a strong place in much of the leadership practice that can be observed currently.

Societies and cultures have changed. Jody often uses the following example in workshops and classes to demonstrate this point.

> When I got my first job, my father told me that whatever the boss told me to do, I was to respond with, "Yes sir!" If he said jump, the proper response was, "How high, sir?" Those were the only responses that demonstrated the proper respect I was to give to the boss.

The benefit for the boss whose employees operated under such a mind-set was obvious—*control*. Many people in leadership positions, as well as those who provide leadership training, believe control remains a major function of the leader. While such logic may seem intuitively correct, research has shown it does not create an environment that facilitates maximum human effectiveness—a culture that encourages open expression of thought, resulting in employee initiative.

The Need for How and Why

Research has conclusively demonstrated the mechanistic style, with its focus on control, constrains creativity, innovation, and productivity. Most importantly, the "how high, sir?" mind-set diminishes the discovery and use of knowledge by the individuals who comprise the work team. The collective intelligence of the group is minimized or not recognized at all.

While the "how high, sir?" mind-set may have been prominent twenty or thirty years ago, it is not as prevalent in today's workforce. Today's workers want to know more about the how and why of a given task.

The Benefit of How and Why

Today's leaders live in an environment that demands reduction of cost and errors and ever-increasing speed. Problem solving and innovation must occur faster in order to maintain a competitive advantage. The flow of information up and down the management levels too often takes an inordinate amount of time, slowing problem solving and mission completion.

Additionally, there is little if any support to show that such approval processes actually improve quality, productivity, error reduction, or customer satisfaction. In practice, what such processes actually do is increase frustration at every level and provide a chain of blame. Common sense encourages us to consider that top-down control and approval systems are a source of waste that can be substantially reduced.

Technical Differences between Mechanistic and CAS Perspectives Are Small but Big

There are several points of difference between the mechanistic and the CAS or holistic perspectives, with "holistic" characterized as bottom-up, collaborative, and big-picture oriented. The leader must be aware of these differences and then strive to create an environment where the most productive conditions can best thrive.

Successful consultant and retired college football coach Tommy Limbaugh compares such an environment to a football huddle. As a coach, Limbaugh teaches, "We are all sweating together, bleeding together, and success requires that we all do our assigned job well, or we all fail; no one person is more important than another."

Continuing the analogy of a huddle, the head coach signals in a play. Meanwhile, the quarterback listens to the wide receiver describe a weakness in the defense. The quarterback simultaneously hears and analyzes the information given by the wide receiver, calls the coach's play, observes the forming line of scrimmage, recognizes defensive weakness, and determines whether an audible (a change to the coach's play) is needed. Ideally, the result is a touchdown. That is the result of collaborative action and emergent thinking.

The first point of difference between the mechanistic and CAS perspectives is the concept of a *semiautonomous agent* (the players in the huddle). The mechanistic system presumes the worker will perform on cue and exactly as expected (run the coach's play). Holistic thinking allows for the reality that those engaged in the work may have different viewpoints or ideas on how to execute a certain process. Or they may have a different understanding of exactly what they are supposed to do. At any given point in time, the agent may *feel* different, affecting his or her level of attention, speed of action, or personal attachment to the ultimate outcome. In that sense, an agent is independent and may exercise varying degrees of autonomy.

Any deviation in action by an agent will have an effect on the immediate and larger system that is *unpredictable*. The effect may be undetectable, minuscule, or highly impactful.

The actions of individual agents, teams, and departments are *interconnected*. In this context, the degree of interconnectedness within a system or set of systems (subsystems that support a larger system—the company) is referred to as *complexity*. Interconnectedness requires communication and collaboration to effectively function. Higher levels of organizational complexity require greater communicative and collaborative effort.

In short, organizations of the twenty-first century operate through agents who are interconnected to varying degrees, which require a high level of communication and collaboration in order to achieve greater effectiveness and continuous improvement.

Diversity of Experience

When a system has agents with many different skills, talents, and experiences, it can be described as rich in *diversity*. Diversity has great value in an organization. Diversity breeds collective wisdom that can be drawn upon for innovation and problem solving. Whenever a team or task force is put together, diversity of function, experience, and viewpoint among the members should be of prime concern.

Constant Change

Within an organization comprised of interconnected semiautonomous agents, the natural result of agent interaction is *constant change*. This is quite the opposite of the "if it ain't broke, don't fix it" mind-set. A growing and dynamic organization is not static or in a state of equilibrium. Continuous improvement requires an environment that is constantly experiencing some change. *Quasi equilibrium* becomes the desirable state.

When an organization is in quasi equilibrium, there may be many small, unspecified changes occurring simultaneously across its subsystems. These changes often occur without any leadership intervention. The issue may have been discovered at the work level and resolved there. Such resolutions are sometimes referred to as *self-directed*.

The system is constantly adapting to these many changes. Such *adaptive changes* can be nonlinear in outcome, meaning the result is exponentially larger or smaller than the apparent action. Small changes at the beginning of a process may result in large, significant changes in final outcome. This is a major reason why abnormalities or defects must be detected and fixed as early as possible in the ongoing production process.

The Edge of Chaos ... in the Zone

At this point, you as the reader may be thinking this entire explanation sounds like chaos. If so, congratulations! This feeling marks the foundational point of understanding modern organizations. The most effective systems operate at the *edge of chaos*.

One's first experience(s) at the edge of chaos may seem uncomfortable and out of control. That discomfort is the door to real performance improvement. Great athletes often talk about being "in the zone." They describe it as being almost out of control—not thinking, just doing. It's a state of consciousness in which the mind is uncluttered and skills are matched to performance with clarity and perfection. The athlete is literally operating at the edge of chaos, trusting her or his skills in the moment to create a positive outcome. This unique blend of power, efficiency, effectiveness, and security is described in the corporate context as *systems fitness*.[2]

The Right Level of Control

It is important to recognize that there is not one right level of control for every system or organization. Organizations may fluctuate between static, edge of chaos, and chaos depending on the life cycles and economic scenarios they face. The leadership challenge will always be to facilitate an environment that enables a dynamic response to the organization's position on the control/emergence continuum.

A leader attempting to nurture a culture of flexible action will encourage agents' ability to intervene meaningfully in the process or processes of which they are part. A classic example of an individual's meaningful intervention is Toyota's *andon* system.[3] *Andon* is a quality assurance mechanism allowing an individual to identify and address a problem at the point of occurrence. In the event an individual worker detects a defect or problem, he or she has the right and obligation to stop the entire process.

The Importance of Shared Assumptions

A prerequisite for well-integrated, semiautonomous agent participation is a set of shared assumptions. Such assumptions include norms for the process, values and beliefs concerning how and why the organization operates in the manner it does, and respect for the integrity and intent of the individual agents. Each agent must be nurtured so that he or she deeply believes in the vision, values and the obligations that accompany those assumptions. Additionally, each agent must believe that following a course of action in line with those assumptions will actually make a difference and improve the performance of the larger team.

It is for this reason the vision and value system of the organization must be an organic part of everyday life for its agents. Semiautonomous action cannot effectively occur without such a binding mechanism.

Just a Few Simple Rules

Lastly, semiautonomous agency best thrives when actions are guided by a few simple rules. The more rules an organization imparts to the individual, the more restricted the individual's activity. Restrictions are the antithesis of flexibility and innovation. Too many companies attempt to solve problems through the creation of rules.

When Jack Welch became CEO of General Electric, one of his first acts was to throw out the company's massive set of rules and procedures. Initially, there were many skeptics, and Welch was nicknamed "Neutron Jack." He realized that rules inhibit creative entrepreneurial action within a company.

When mistakes or problems occur, the creation of preventative rules may seem like the quickest and best remedy, but such rulemaking has a way of rebounding to deliver unintended consequences. An organization of any size is always better served by solving the problem at the point of action. Dr. Jeffrey Liker, in his book *The Toyota Way*, emphasizes this as a basic philosophy at Toyota.[4]

A Learning Organization

Organizations tend to revert to current or original patterns of behavior. Leaders must be sensitive to this reality and constantly push agents to stretch their comfort zones. This cannot simply be mandated with any hope of long-term success. It is best encouraged through learning.

A learning organization strives to develop and implement policies and strategies that make use of the learning at every level of the organization. Leaders who open the doors of learning through company-sponsored initiatives send the message that new ideas are wanted and needed. The cutting edge will not be achieved and cannot be sustained by an "if it ain't broke, don't fix it" or "this is the way we have always done it" mind-set.

Some companies are reluctant to learn from organizations outside their particular industry. For whatever reasons, their leaders believe that their industry operates in such a unique manner that practices from unaffiliated industries have little useful application to their situation.

The field of hospital administration is an example of an industry using the ideas of other industries to overcome its problems. Aware of rising costs, hospitals have embraced the *lean* concept to help identify waste. The term *lean* identifies an enterprise that strives to optimize value created for a customer, within a supply chain, through the minimization of time, cost, and errors (when speaking of this concept, the term will be italicized so as to eliminate confusion with the adjective lean).[5] Nurses have applied *lean* concepts to the problems of human error. Hospitals with a *lean* emphasis use sophisticated methods of transferring patient treatment responsibilities and information between the various disciplines and departments. A review of the current literature on *lean* indicates that production concepts drawn from the automobile industry can be meaningfully applied to the field of medicine, resulting in significant improvement.

Embracing a new logic of leadership requires the recognition that all organizations are complex and operate by CAS characteristics. Positive change occurs when a leader understands those characteristics and then adjusts to find the balancing point between appropriate control and emergent behavior.

From Worst to First

One of the best examples of how this adaptive, self-directed method works is, of all places, the military's current approach to leadership. This is highly evident among the military elites (Rangers, SEALs, Special Forces) and the navy, as described by Captain David Marquet in his book *Turn the Ship Around* (2012) and Captain Michael Abrashoff in *It's Our Ship* (2008).

The navy has a long and proud history of employing the concept of an all-powerful, absolutely controlling ship's captain. Make no mistake: the captain of a US naval vessel remains absolutely accountable for the mission of the ship, the ship itself, and the men and women onboard. As Captains Marquet's and Abrashoff's true accounts demonstrate, the top-down control methods of the past are changing, with astounding results.

You Did What?

Captain Marquet was selected to command a US Navy ballistic missile submarine, specifically the USS *Olympia*. He underwent one full year of study and training about that specific ship. Each of the forty-one ballistic missile submarines in the US Navy is unique in systems and layout. The reason for their differences is that it takes a long time to build such a ship, and technological advances occur at varied rates. Therefore, there may be significant changes between the building of the first ship of a certain class and the building of the fourth.

Despite the year of boat-specific preparation for the *Olympia*, Captain Marquet was ultimately given command of the USS *Santa Fe*. The *Santa Fe* held the distinction of having the lowest performance rating in the Pacific Fleet at that time. Captain Marquet faced a daunting challenge: he was assuming command of a ship with a history of poor performance and low morale, and he was unfamiliar with the ship's unique systems. Marquet was forced to operate in a manner that went against the prevailing culture of that ship and of the navy as a whole. Because he did not possess the desirable level of systems familiarity, he was forced to ask many questions when problems arose, instead of giving the expected directive solutions. "Rather than telling everyone what they needed to do, I would ask questions about how they thought we should approach the problem."[6]

Problems arose among the ranks. The pace of decision-making on a ballistic missile submarine often does not allow time for team discussion. Marquet had to devise a culture that encouraged individual crewmembers and units to solve issues as they arose, without his direct input. "We deconstructed decision authority and pushed it down to where the information lived."[7] It was a necessary experiment that took courage and carried career risk.

The outcome was revolutionary, taking the crew of the *Santa Fe* from worst to first in less than a year. The *Santa Fe* experiment proved to Captain Marquet and the navy that the human capital on a submarine is undoubtedly the ship's most precious resource. Such a remarkable accomplishment merited examination by the navy and certainly makes a worthwhile case study for organizational leaders at all levels.

Captain Marquet observed that the crew of the *Santa Fe* had become so focused on results and not making mistakes that section leaders were fearful of action. He needed to change the mind-set of the boat's midlevel leaders. He needed them to focus on process, always doing their best, and continual improvement rather than immediate results. He encouraged them to think freely and creatively within the operating restrictions of a particular system, always prepared to make a best-scenario recommendation.

In effect, leader-to-leader relationships were created between midlevel leaders, rather than exclusive leader-to-follower relationships between captain and subordinates. Captain Marquet found he was not controlling decisions and actions, but allowing them to emerge through the collaborative sharing of critical knowledge in an ongoing manner.

He even changed the way decisions were communicated. Department heads and operational leaders stated to him, "Captain, I intend to steer 150 degrees at a depth of 200 feet," instead of waiting for the captain to say, "Make your depth 200 feet and steer 150 degrees." If the captain agreed with the expressed intention, he would simply say, "Carry on." Such a simple but dramatically different method of communicating completely changed the mind-set and actions of the crew.

The results achieved by Captain Marquet and the crew of the Santa Fe confirm the CAS theories expounded by Drs. Choi and Dooley. They concluded that emergent patterns of behavior can be much more effectively managed through positive feedback. Managers must learn to appropriately balance the desire to control with the need to let solutions emerge.[8]

Dr. Barbara Kellerman uses the term *leader/follower continuum* rather than leader-to-leader, but both phrases describe the same phenomenon.[9] Leaders and followers achieve greater creativity in solving problems and increasing productivity when they morph between the roles of leader and follower, based upon the particular situation and levels of specific knowledge.

Marquet demonstrated that a collaborative, leader-to-leader style can achieve exemplary results without sacrificing balance. He embraced the emergent outcomes with faith in the collective wisdom of his team.

Success Is a Team Sport

Captain Abrashoff came to similar conclusions, but arrived at them from a completely different perspective. He confesses early on in his book that he made the mistake of thinking of the USS *Benfold* (a destroyer) as his sole responsibility, the source of his identity, and not thinking enough about the rest of the battle group. "I should have realized that the *Benfold* would succeed only as part of its battle group, and that I didn't have a monopoly on great ideas."[10] He came to understand that other ships were doing things that he had never thought of and would never hear about because he hadn't created a trusting forum for the exchange of information.

Internal competition, so often the lifeblood of existence for Western organizations, can have many positive outcomes, but it can also significantly hinder the sharing of ideas. Many companies love to stack-rank every management measurement—sales, costs, error rates, productivity, days without reportable accidents, profitability. Certainly, organizations need to keep a close eye on these important benchmarks, but ranking offices, departments, or individuals can cause serious issues for a collaborative environment.

If my department is ahead of yours, and we are both competing for the same promotion, there is a dilemma. What will happen if I share my good idea with you (good for the company), and then you beat me (bad for my dreams of promotion)? This simple example demonstrates how pay and promotion practices can be completely out of step with maximum organizational effectiveness.

In the case of Captain Abrashoff, he was an impediment to maximum performance of the battle group. Fortunately, he learned that if the battle group was defeated, he might die. There are too many leaders in corporate America who are similar impediments. In a collaborative leader-to-leader style or leader/follower continuum, the measure of performance becomes the continuous improvement of the whole. Thinking of leadership from that perspective opens up a whole new set of performance possibilities.

The examples of the football huddle, Captain Marquet on the USS *Santa Fe*, and Captain Abrashoff on the USS *Benfold* confirm that real success begins with the realization that the good of the team must come first. Leaders must recognize that their needs are not necessarily congruent with what is best for the team. Effective leaders throughout history have demonstrated that the welfare of the people must come before the needs and glory of the leader. Regardless of whether we are speaking in terms of organizations, ships, or football teams, the long-term winners realize we are all in it together.

Exercises for Reflection and Learning

1. Can players call an audible in your organization? If so, what are the boundaries for such action? Are those boundaries broad enough to allow for real impact?
2. The following characteristics are critical for maximizing the performance of any organization (CAS):
    - bottom-up flow of information
    - collaboration across all structural boundaries
    - team-first perspective
    - diversification of experience
    - freedom to challenge the status quo
    - balance of control (control versus emergence)
    - a few simple rules
    - shared assumptions (vision and values)
    - learning organization
    - courage to operate at the edge of chaos

As a team, evaluate your organization by rating each characteristic on a scale of one to ten (one being poor and ten being optimal). Repeat the process, considering the ideal rating for your specific organization. Analyze the differences and determine a plan of action to approach the ideal.

SECTION 2

The Leadership Drought espouses six distinct leadership principles. We define a *principle* as a universal ingredient required in the practice of leadership, one that should never be violated. Many different techniques may be employed in the application of those six principles, but every organization or team aspiring to greatness must have these characteristic ingredients.

Current realities are far too complex and fast-moving to be effectively coordinated by mechanistic (top-down) managers. Great organizations must be collaborative, able to rapidly summon collective knowledge, and flexible enough to respond in the moment. Such capabilities do not just happen. They are ingrained in team members through the six principles.

These six principles are as follows:

- common personal awareness
- shared vision of a desired future
- team-first mentality
- leader/follower commitment
- continuous improvement as a way of life
- delegation as the primary tool of leadership development

Each principle builds upon the others. They should be encountered in sequence. Maximum effectiveness prohibits the standard procedure of cherry-picking. At the end of section 2, the reader will have an understanding of the principles along with some techniques for learning and implementation.

3

THE FIRST PRINCIPLE: BECOMING AWARE

> Without self-awareness, you cannot understand your strengths
> and weakness, your "super powers" versus your "kryptonite."
> —A. Tjan, R. Harrington, T. Hsieh

Who Am I? How Do I Think?

Howard Gardner, in his book *Extraordinary Minds,* concludes that exceptional people have an "exceptional talent for identifying their own strengths and weaknesses."[1] The unfortunate fact, however, is that most people are terrible at estimating their abilities. Dr. Carol Dweck has done significant research on this subject. Her findings indicate that people continue to misevaluate their own performance and abilities.[2] When she attempted to discover why this was so, she uncovered a golden nugget of information. People who have what she calls a "learning mindset" go against the trend and prove very accurate in self-assessment.[3]

Dr. Dweck describes the learning mind-set as a personal belief in one's ability to develop a cherished quality through focused effort and perseverance. The ability to stick to it, especially when the process is not going well, is the hallmark of the mind-set.[4]

Not all people see their lives in such a manner. There are many who perceive life somewhat like a poker game: the choice is playing the hand dealt or folding. Dweck's insight is an exciting revelation—leaders are learners!

The first step toward living as a continuous learner is the recognition of personal ignorance, or awareness of what one doesn't know. Once that reality sets in, the task becomes gaining information. As information is collected and energy is invested, thought, knowledge, and wisdom are created, which are the birth of innovation. Once that epiphany occurs and the innovative process is initiated, personal transformation can take hold, resulting in a positive upward spiral of confidence.[5] (See "The Positive Spiral of Innovative Experience" figure below.)

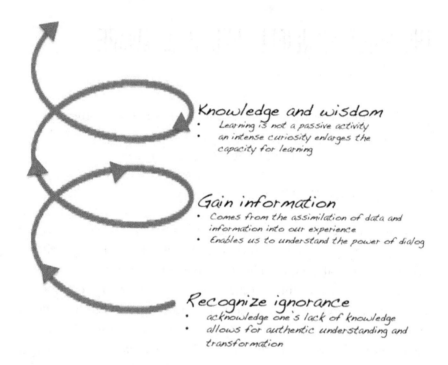

Knowledge and wisdom
- Learning is not a passive activity
- an intense curiosity enlarges the capacity for learning

Gain information
- Comes from the assimilation of data and information into our experience
- Enables us to understand the power of dialog

Recognize ignorance
- acknowledge one's lack of knowledge
- allows for authentic understanding and transformation

My Built-In Filters and Traps

Every person gathers a set of filters, as they move through that phenomenon known as life. People soak up beliefs from parents, family, and close friends. This process begins at the moment of earliest remembrance. These beliefs may also be called a person's prejudices. Prejudices may or may not be accurate, but they do impact everyday actions and decisions, acting as screens for how information and observations are understood. (See "Information Filters" figure shown on next page.)

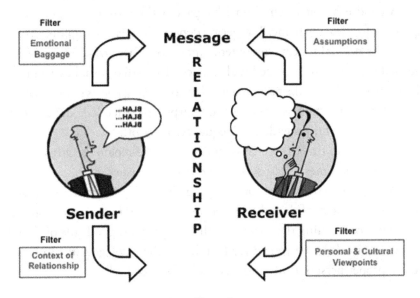

Prejudice always leads to assumption, but not all assumptions are as ingrained as prejudices. An assumption can be described as decision or action taken without prerequisite thought. Experienced leaders can fall prey to the problem of assumption: "I have seen this situation hundreds of times, and the outcome is always the same, so let's just ..." Fortunately, their experience usually serves them well. But this habit of thought completely discounts that moment when something is different and real change may be imminent.

The good news about assumptions is that, once these are recognized, people can usually adapt and act accordingly, if it is not too late or the situation dire.

Everyday living is a chronicle of encounters and experiences of the day. Human beings tend to carry those encounters like baggage, toting them around from meeting to meeting, hour after hour. Some are discarded as the day goes on, and some stay in the bag longer. Emotional baggage is thus in constant change. It has the potential to impact activities throughout the daily experience. While the lifespan of an individual item in the bag may be short, its impact can be long-lasting if, say, the dirty underwear is exposed in the wrong circumstance.

A good example of emotional baggage is the proverbial fight with a spouse before leaving home. The person departs the scene of unpleasantness, upset, the normal routine disrupted. Upon his or her arrival at the office, normal greetings are replaced with silence or less-than-usual exuberance. The person addresses the tasks at hand, but something goes wrong. Reaction becomes overreaction. Colleagues are surprised, offended, defensive. A chain reaction of unintended consequences is set off.

Most of the time, these consequences can be repaired. Other times, such action becomes a "last straw," and conflict ensues.

While this type of emotional baggage is usually the most short-lived of a person's habits of thought, leaders must attempt to maintain constant awareness concerning the content of their baggage. A good rule of thumb is not to let others see your dirty laundry. If the baggage gets too heavy, seek a proper person, time, and place for "show and tell."

Personality

In the context of leadership, the term *personality* includes every factor that describes one's values, sensitivities, goals, habits, and inclinations for coping with the vast spectrum of situations leaders face.[6] Each of the factors communicates a message from the leader. Perceptions are created based upon those messages, some right and some not so right. Regardless of the level of correctness, those messages/perceptions are the real truth for the observer. They remain intact until the leader proves differently through subsequent actions.

A major point in understanding effective leadership is seeing it as a communication process. Each decision, action, question, and instruction becomes a commentary about who the leader really is and her or his real purpose. The conscious act of leading places an individual in an intimate state of being. Each thought and action reflects the values and beliefs that inform the leader's thinking. All observed actions convey some meaning to those who see and hear. What was seen and heard impacts the followers' thinking and subsequent actions. The various perceived meanings might involve motivation, purpose, or some implied "coded" message.

The recent efforts of Hillary Clinton, in her quest to become president, demonstrate this human tendency very well. She continually made statements crafted to appeal to the studied wants and desires of selected constituencies. Yet the polls continued to indicate broad distrust among voters and a level of perceived insincerity in the candidate. It remains difficult to know if her comments arose from deep conviction; an effort to capture the "magic" of her husband, former President Bill Clinton; or direction from political advisers. Her many changes on specific positions tended to diminish the possibility of voters developing deep conviction.

Unfortunately for Clinton, too many people perceived her words and actions as attempts to copy thoughts that were not hers. She was not seen as genuine. Her words were not in harmony with her situation. As Shakespeare admonished, one must be true to one's own self.[7] A leader must act in concert with his or her own personality and value set to be perceived as genuine and sincere.

A leader carries the burden of constant observation. He or she is always "onstage" and the subject of judgment. With that burden must come the realization that everyone is influenced by personal biases and prejudices. Every leader communicates to the world through a particular set of filters. Individuals likewise receive the message through their own filters. Often the communication is misunderstood, resulting in a wide variation in perceptions and actions among those receiving the message.

As a leader, one must constantly remind oneself that everything one does is an act of communication. This point should be like an electric shock, instantly gaining attention and provoking a few vitally important questions. What message will the observers take away? Will they apply the leader's intended meaning or some derivative? Does the takeaway message clearly describe the meaning(s) intended and facilitate the desired action?

Think, Then Act: Performance Will Be Congruent

Thinking is the first step and prerequisite action for all leadership. Prerequisite thinking should not only consider the words contained in the message, but the best medium for conveyance and the tone of delivery. All of these things can add or take away from the urgency and importance of the message.

Tone and Priority

The leader must be fully aware that personality has tone and impacts how people perceive every message, especially any sense of urgency. In the book *Achieving Leadership Genius,* the authors make a distinction between *disposition-driven behavior* and *value-driven behavior.* They point out that much of our behavior is instinctive and therefore without regard for consciously intended outcomes, sometimes causing uncomfortable or dysfunctional situations. They classify instinct as *disposition-driven* behavior.[8]

Ideally, the leader seeks to create a compatible environment where there is free flow of thought and high levels of understanding. When people find themselves uncomfortable, especially if that discomfort causes a sense of threat, communication is hindered and actions will vary from hoped-for outcomes.

How can a leader improve compatibility and comfort in a given encounter? The answer leads to *value-driven behavior,* or mindful behavior based upon a set of values rather than actions driven by instinct.

Personality Assessment

The personality assessment process is a proven means of helping people become more aware of their predispositions in thought and behavior (disposition-driven tendencies). This kind of awareness confronts a person with the realities of her or his personal impact on and compatibility with other people.

Upon grasping this point, leaders quickly realize the missed opportunities and reasons for conflict they have experienced in the past. Typically they hunger for deep understanding because they recognize the potential for improvement in communication, personal interaction, and diversity of thought.

DiSC

There are many personality assessments available in the marketplace. Most are based on the earliest foundational research of Carl Jung (1923) and William Marston (1929). We chose to use the DiSC model for the purpose of discussion because it is application-focused for leaders and managers, making the language more compatible.[9] Additionally, DiSC offers a full suite of compatible assessments on teamwork, innovation, and leadership assessment tools (often referred to as "360" assessment).

Many people have been exposed to the DiSC model and proudly proclaim their assessed style. Like the authors of *Achieving Leadership Genius*, we prefer that readers focus less on the labels (*D*, *i*, *S*, and *C*) and more on the behavioral patterns exhibited by the various basic styles. Those basic styles are: Dominance, Influence, Steadiness, and Conscientiousness.

Understanding the DiSC model allows a leader to be more acutely aware of personal behavior. More importantly, it increases a leader's ability to modify that behavior appropriately, facilitating a more comfortable and open environment. When team members feel comfortable and open, the effectiveness of communication is greatly enhanced.

William Marston conducted the research and developed the foundations for the DiSC model. He was a lawyer, psychologist, and inventor—he invented the first lie detector, known as the polygraph. His studies led him to believe that people have core tendencies in behavior that becomes set very early in life, around the age of five years. This basic disposition is normally referred to as one's personality.

Core tendencies do not change easily. When change does occur, it is usually the result of traumatic experience. Examples include near-death experience, the death of a deeply loved person, a particularly rough divorce, or getting fired from a job that impacts personal identity.

Personality Does Not Change; Modification Is Temporary

At this point of discussion, an important distinction must be made. There is a major difference between a psychological change in personality and the development of flexibility to modify one's actions for a particular purpose. When a person modifies his or her normal behavior to create a more inviting, open, and comfortable environment, basic personality does not change. Specific behavioral tendencies are consciously modified for a temporary period. This point will become clearer as the discussion progresses.

Marston believed that personal tendencies develop along the same patterns as fight-or-flight theories. Based upon a person's early experiences, certain aspects of the survival instinct become hardwired into the unconscious mind. The sense of conflict and perceived ability to control the immediate environment develop based upon observation and personal experience.

As these unconscious beliefs are confirmed through further observation and experience, a persona emerges that reflect that person's deep-seated strategy for survival. There are two primary axes upon which the strategy can be measured: confront conflict or try to avoid it, and control the situation (extroversion) or adapt to it (introversion).

Practical Application of the DiSC Model

The process for effectively using the DiSC model has three steps:

1. Understand yourself (learn the tendencies of your style).
2. Learn to recognize the predominant style of those you encounter.
3. Modify your tendencies so that your desired outcome (effective communication) is more fully understood through the personality styles of those you are trying communicate with.

Recognizing the Predominant Style of Those You Meet

Observe the person with whom you are interacting and then ask two questions. (See "People's Environmental Relationship" figure shown on next page.)

1. Is the person introverted or extroverted? If there are not enough clues to make that determination, consider pace, or how fast the person processes information or moves. If the person is extroverted or tends to move and think more quickly, she or he is likely D or i (the two styles above the horizontal line in the chart). If a person's pace is more moderate, she or he is likely C or S (the two styles below the horizontal line in the chart).
2. Does the person attempt to control the situation or environment, or does the person tend to be more adaptive? If a person tends

toward controlling, he or she is either *D* or *C* (the two styles on the left side of the vertical line in the chart). If a person appears to be more adaptive to the situation, he or she is likely *i* or *S* (the two styles on the right side of the vertical line in the chart).

People's Environmental Relationship

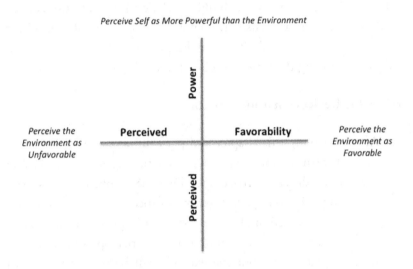

Perceive Self as More Powerful than the Environment

Perceive the Environment as Unfavorable — **Perceived** | **Favorability** — *Perceive the Environment as Favorable*

Power

Perceived

Perceive Self as Less Powerful than the Environment

Experiment with the chart. With just a little practice and the information contained in appendix B, "DiSC Characteristics," you can become quite adept at recognition of DiSC style.

Modifying Your Tendencies for Improved Communication

Armed with the information from a personal DiSC assessment and the ability to recognize other styles in people, a skilled communicator can begin to modify instinctive behaviors, offering a more congruent and relaxing style suited to the environment. Practice this skill—it will be worth your time!

Some people may learn to modify their behavioral tendencies without the use of DiSC or other assessments. Experience teaches us what works and doesn't work, and how to approach different people differently. This process is called *maturity*.

The problem with learning by maturation is that it takes a lifetime. Being more aware of oneself and of others in any given context can provide a younger leader with a significant edge in establishing relationships and building trust.

Scholars are fond of saying that building relationships and trust requires long periods of time. Leaders usually do not have the luxury of time. Great leaders have the uncanny ability to make people feel comfortable and relaxed, thus reducing the time needed to build relationships and trust.

Exercises for Reflection and Learning

1. After reviewing this chapter and performing a DiSC assessment for each team member, conduct a practice session on leadership behavior modification based upon DiSC. (See appendix C, "GAPS Coaching.") Encourage the sharing of specific ideas about how a modified approach might open a door or improve a relationship.
2. Conduct a leadership communication workshop. You may have to hire a facilitator, but the exercise will be more than worth it. The first goal of the workshop is to make everyone aware of their personal tendencies (values, filters, personality). Encourage discussion about the potential impact for improved communication and engagement with their immediate associates and the larger organization. The second goal is to encourage thought and discussion about how this knowledge can help employees answer three important questions:
    *   What is my leader's commitment to excellence?
    *   Can I trust my leader?
    *   Does my leader care about me?

4

THE SECOND PRINCIPLE: SHARED VISION, DESIRED FUTURE

> Where there is no vision, the people perish.
> —Proverbs 29:18

Vision—A Misunderstood Idea

Proverbs 29:18 may be one of the most misapplied verses in the Bible. The concept is often used by churches and other organizations for the purpose of establishing a specific goal and an organized plan for achievement. Consultants involved in the vision businesses often quote the verse.

While the idea is worthwhile for these and many other possible reasons, it was not the true intent of the Hebrew author. The author's original intent was to warn of the total loss of social order if the values and guidelines of the prophets were not followed. The people would run wild, out of control, without direction. The verse warned that long-term triumph would not be achieved if certain guidelines and boundaries were not observed.

The verse does not apply to the task of creating a vision. The existing vision meets the need for guidance, supporting values, and boundaries, which are vital to the life of the community.[1] The biblical concept suggests that the ideal desired future will only be achieved if the pathway is understood and the people comply with the agreed-upon rules and boundaries (values).

The biblical sense of "vision" holds a much deeper meaning than we often attribute to the fancy words on brass plates that adorn organizational walls. The original meaning places the vision far above the fluff, as many leaders now perceive it, and into the category of absolute necessity.

33

The Vision Provides for a Common Goal

A distinguished philosopher wrote that the greatest force for the advancement of the human species is "a great hope held in common."[2] Burt Nanus, professor of management at the University of Southern California, teaches that effective leadership requires a commitment to the success of every individual in the organization. Every individual must be taught how to constantly improve their ability to accomplish a common goal.[3] Everyone who works under the banner of a vision must find personal value and hope for a better future. Norman Vincent Peale believed, first and foremost, that leadership is about adding value to people.[4]

In organizational development terms, such a common goal would typically be called the vision. More specifically, it would be a shared vision; individual goals and the organizational goals are in sync and aligned. The shared vision represents the core motivational philosophy of the organization. Through the vision, each member of the organization has a clear sense of purpose: where the organization is going, and the behaviors and guidelines that will mark the way. The shared vision is relatable to every position, from CEO to the lowest-level team member. It can be directly applied to every decision for the purpose of ascertaining validity, correctness, and priority. In essence, every action and decision should be justifiable by the vision.

Potential Value of a Shared Vision

Many question the usefulness of a vision and the visioning process as a tool for organizational accomplishment. The vision statement is perceived as fluff and of little measurable value. Companies whose leaders have no vision are doomed to function under the burden of mere tradition. Such leaders limit innovation and growth, because they are reduced to keeping things as things have always been. They seem to be guided by the premise "if it ain't broke, don't fix it" or the ubiquitous "this is the way we have always done it."

Research completed in 2014 by Jing, Avery, and Bergsteiner found that when leaders actively work with a vision, improved outcomes in the form of employee and customer satisfaction, productivity, employee retention, and financial success occur throughout the organization.[5]

No Commitment—No Vision

Most organizations, especially the big and well known, have vision statements hewn in stone or polished brass and prominently placed on marble walls for all to see. Some even print the vision on the back of business cards, arguably to impress clients and potential customers. They all are eloquently wordsmithed but, unfortunately, have little or no impact on employees' daily activities.

If the reader would like to test this claim, simply ask anyone in a company to recite word for word, from memory, the organizational vision statement. If you want to supplement your income, bring some twenty-dollar bills with you and add a bet to the challenge. The usual response is "I can tell you what it generally says," followed by "Why does it have to be word for word?"

That is an excellent question. It leads to a deeper understanding of what an effective vision is and the level of commitment required to make it a cultural reality. Properly used, the vision becomes a constant reminder to all employees that they are part of a purpose that is bigger than themselves. It provides a guideline for every choice that supports that purpose.

Jack Welch, the former CEO of General Electric, is considered controversial by some, but few deny that he was very effective. Much has been written about his "Eight Rules for Leaders." The second rule is "Leaders make sure people not only see the vision, they live and breathe it."[6]

Why Is a Vision Important?

The vision is important for several reasons. First, it empowers courage of action. Every person on the team knows the overall purpose of their activity and should use the vision as a means of justification for every action. If a contemplated action cannot be justified by the vision, then such action should not be taken—or, at least, it should be reconsidered. The vision plays a part in hiring, training, coaching, counseling, sales, marketing, and asset allocation. It becomes imprinted on the hearts and souls of every employee.

Second, a well-constructed vision enables sound prioritization, in keeping with the overall objectives of the organization. Everyone in the organization should be looking and thinking ahead, not just the leaders.

There must be a big picture visible to each team member. The clearer the big-picture priorities, the better the resulting decisions at all levels.

The Italian economist Pareto supposedly once said, if you are Noah, and your ark is about to sink, look for the elephants first, because you can throw over a bunch of cats and dogs and squirrels and everything else that is just a small animal—and your ark will continue to sink. We're not sure if Pareto actually made the comment, but regardless, it remains a great example. How often have all of us seen the scuttling of cats and dogs in an effort to save the organizational elephants?

Third, vision is useful in the selection and retention of people. When the vision is an intrinsic part of everyday life, it becomes like a line in the sand. Explaining the organizational vision with job candidates serves multiple purposes. If an individual wants to be a part of the team, she or he must make a conscious decision concerning the journey together. Along with that decision comes an expectation of how every member will act in pursuit of that desired future. This guiding rule remains in force during the entire term of one's contract with the organization. If people can no longer abide by those terms, they are obliged to remove themselves from participation. The vision interfaces with training, coaching, counseling, and, when necessary, termination.

When the vision is intrinsic to daily life in the organization, it becomes the foundation for trust building in many types of organizational relationships. It is the measure of conduct and proper decision-making. It stands as the ultimate authority.

Vision or Shared Vision

The concept of a vision has been around for a long time. Recall the Bible verse with which we kicked off this chapter. Harvard professor John Kotter has observed many companies' efforts to achieve organizational transformation. The companies that attempt change from an authoritarian perspective (mechanistic or top-down) tend to achieve little more than maintenance of the existing system. Kotter's conclusion is that the only meaningful approach to change begins with a vision developed through collaboration among the many levels of an organization. It is hard work, often messy (two steps forward and one step back), and takes time.[7] It really can't be done by direction from the CEO, lengthy PowerPoint presentations, and a rollout.

Kotter further explains that change programs never work well over the long run unless they are guided by a vision that appeals to most of the people who have a stake in the enterprise.[8] A shared vision creates a commonality of interest that enables people to see meaning and coherence in the diverse activities of the typical workday.[9] An effective vision does not reflect the narrow desires of a small constituency. An effective vision reflects the shared long-term interests of a broad and perhaps diverse constituency, never trampling on the needs of any stakeholders.

Righteous Action—The End Does Not Justify the Means

The shared vision should be the ultimate authority and justification for all organizational action. It provides the reasoning and shield for unpopular or difficult decisions, when leadership is questioned. The practice of *connective alignment* demonstrates that every employee thinks and acts within the same context of purpose. Everyone rows in the same direction, using the same size oar. This is not about compliance with another set of rules, but a psychological commitment to a purpose greater than self.

The end does not justify the means. Every action must be judged on its own merit. Without connective alignment with the vision, justification falls away, leaving full responsibility attached to the decision maker. Such a situation does not automatically result in censure, but it does focus the spotlight of inquiry.

John Maxwell provides a rarely considered but extremely valuable context for righteous action and the vision. In his book *Good Leaders Ask Great Questions*, he describes how his father always advised him and his siblings to treat other people not as they are, but how they could be.[10]

The impact of this truth has been proven many times in research concerning school children. Varied projects have conclusively shown that people rise to their level of treatment. A well-developed vision describes the organization, the people, and all who are associated in terms of what they can ideally become. It clearly articulates how every team member will be respected and treated. The well-constructed vision brings thoroughly researched theory and practice into a full circle of reality.

Does Your Organization Need a New Vision?

Vision always deals with the future. The vision is where tomorrow begins. The right vision is an idea so energizing that it can effectively jump-start the future by calling forth skills, talents, and resources now dormant or atrophied.[11] The possibility of new opportunity for development and prosperity lifts the level of excitement, raising the dead to new life.

Certainly every new start-up business venture needs a vision as a guidepost for effort. Throughout the life cycle of every organization, rapid changes in innovation, cultural preferences, and industry maturation present the need to review and rethink direction. Sooner or later, the time will come when the organization needs redirection or perhaps complete transformation.[12] Burt Nanus listed some warning signs that arise when a new vision is needed:

- evidence of confusion about purpose or direction
- frequent disagreement among key people concerning priorities, opportunities, or threats
- pessimism or cynicism—people aren't having fun doing their jobs anymore
- loss of market share or reputation
- stakeholders suggest the organization is slipping
- decline in employee pride—people are just working for their checks
- unusual risk avoidance and finger-pointing
- lack of positive feeling concerning the future
- questions about whether people still trust and respect top management[13]

The leader, whether a CEO or team leader, should always begin with the shared vision of the stakeholders as the first step toward revitalization.

Basic Steps in Creation of a Shared Vision

Step 1: Communicate what is happening
- clear and concise description of purpose
- importance and desired impact
- description of process
- selection of coordinating committee and small drafting groups, including a cross-section of the organization

Step 2: Begin the information-gathering process
- simultaneous small group settings
- survey
- discussion
- groups craft their thoughts into a rough draft, based on an example format
- collect the notes and drafts

Step 3: Share the drafts for cross-pollination
- the coordinating committee provides copies to each group, from each group, for review by all
- groups refine their drafts and return second drafts to the coordinating committee

Step 4: Coordinating committee synthesizes the input
- the committee develops a list of the most often-mentioned points

Step 5: Circulate the common points
- groups review and rank the points
- rankings are submitted back to coordinating committee

Step 6: Craft the proposed thoughts into vision form
- coordinating committee composes a draft of the collective vision
- draft is circulated among senior leadership for comment

Step 7: Guidelines for draft review
- Does this vision reflect the thoughts of all stakeholders?

- Are there any critical gaps or overreaches?

Step 8: Draft the final proposal
- coordinating committee produces a polished statement reflecting the thoughts and dreams of the stakeholders
- committee established the percentage of acceptance that will constitute ratification

Step 9: Ratification
- the small groups who wrote the original drafts review the final and vote for acceptance or nonacceptance
- the vote tallies are submitted to the coordinating committee

Step 10: Presentation, Celebration, and Allegiance
- the presentation of a new vision statement should have major-event status
- explain how the vision will benefit every stakeholder
- senior leadership demonstrates allegiance to the vision
- present each employee with a laminated wallet copy

How Long Will It Take?

Crafting a new vision will take as long as it takes! The objections that arise to an elongated process are legion. Not all CFOs and accountants will happily embrace the time and resource expenditure.

The process does provide a fresh vision, built from the input of all parties and therefore supplying at least a modicum of buy-in. When approached openly and sincerely, this process can provide a level of passion—at least from some—that cannot be quantified on the balance sheet. How many passionate people does it take to start a movement? Yes, it is "sunk" money, but at least the money was sunk in the hearts and minds of the people who can make the vision happen.

Living and Breathing the Vision in Daily Life

Have you ever known or observed someone who has a high level of passion for an idea? Such people are usually very compelling, even when others disagree with their position. Human beings are drawn to those who exhibit passion. Leaders who take groups to new heights of accomplishment display passion for the endeavor. They paint a picture with their words that attracts people and makes them want to be a part of the vision.

The first step for any leader trying to awaken his or her team is to gain attention with a compelling picture of what the future could hold. Make that vision a part of every encounter from this point forward. That may sound a bit over the top, but it is not! Yes, the leader risks becoming a Johnny One Note, but that is exactly what it takes to infuse the vision into the minds of the team. The picture must be painted over and over again until every team member knows it by heart. A well-articulated shared vision will become the reference point of every action.

Research by Associate Professor Adam Grant of the Wharton School demonstrated that leaders who encourage discussion and put a face on the vision enhance the vision's meaningfulness. Such contact overcomes the problem of employees wondering if the vision truly has meaning or is merely rhetoric.[14] The real-life message is that the vision does provide meaning to work, especially when the vision is directly connected to and reinforced through real stories of people who have worked under its guidance.

The bottom line: the leader needs to speak about the vision and connect daily circumstances with the vision whenever possible.

Hiring through the Vision

A clear and succinct organizational vision serves as a wonderful tool in the hiring process. Set aside a block of time early in the process to discuss the vision in detail. Highlight the purpose of each phrase. Explain how the concepts connect and help create the organization's culture and desired outcomes.

Emphasis at this point in the employee relationship demonstrates the centrality of the vision and the set of accompanying values. The candidate should be encouraged to consider the vision and values seriously and certify her or his willingness to be a part of the cultural focus. The candidate should clearly understand that all she or he does will be judged by this code.

Counseling and Coaching through the Vision

Every leader in the organization must make themselves familiar with how the vision and values apply to each and every position within their areas of responsibility. In this way, the vision becomes the mirror through which the organization judges itself. Every evaluative encounter, from coaching to remedial counseling, should directly relate to and be discussed through the lens of the vision.

For example, a statement within the vision that "*we are the industry leader in* exceeding *customer expectations*" has several underlying requirements that are incumbent on performance. These requirements would obviously be the minimum standards and expectations for a given position. A supervisor fully aligned in his or her coaching efforts would ascertain if an employee knows the specific expectations of each customer and has a plan to exceed those expectations. Such a line of inquiry will inevitably lead to productive direction.

The Vision as the Basis for Reward and Recognition

A good vision statement helps bind a culture when used in the expression of appreciation and recognition. Referring again to the example of "*we are the industry leader in* exceeding *customer expectations*," a leader wishing to express appreciation when a customer comments about a certain department exceeding expectations might use the following technique:

> I want to **thank** (person, team, department). ABC, Inc. expressed their pleasure (**observed/heard**) in the way you expedited their recent order. This **demonstrates** your commitment and adherence to our vision, specifically exceeding customer expectations. We **appreciate** your effort and want **you** to know that your effort made a difference today!

Use the TODAY method to provide immediate and beneficial recognition to deserving personnel.

T   I want to take this moment to *THANK YOU* _____.

O   I *OBSERVED* (or heard) you doing _____.

D   In doing _____ you *DEMONSTRATED* _____.

A   We all *APPRECIATE* your efforts _____.

Y   *YOU MADE A DIFFERENCE* by doing _____ today!

Reference to the vision when giving recognition truly helps to instill the vision in the minds of the people who are the organization. They hear it when things are going well, and it is referenced when things do not go well. The repetitive exposure imprints the vision on the collective mind-set of the organization. Slowly but surely, the vision becomes part of everyday thoughts and actions at all levels. The vision literally becomes the foundation on which the organization builds.

The Vision as a Basis for Termination

When the vision is actively communicated throughout the business process, it also provides significant benefit in termination situations. Leaders discussing the reason(s) for dismissal can relate the reason to the vision and stay away from comments of a personal nature. This practice tends to maintain an atmosphere of respect for the individual and a higher level of professionalism within the company, thus reducing the possibility of legal recourse for improper termination.

Exercises for Reflection and Learning

1. Ask the leaders of your organization the following two questions:
   - How would your job as leader be different if we operated according to a well-constructed, well-communicated, and fully integrated vision?
   - What do the answers to the above question indicate?

2. Using small group forums, have a discussion concerning the following:
   - Would the existence of a well-constructed and well-communicated vision have the potential for improving decision-making at the lowest levels of the organization?
   - Would a well-constructed vision offer a big picture that could help overcome misunderstanding and miscommunication at the various levels of the organization?
   - Would a well-constructed vision facilitate improved performance, evaluation, and recognition procedures by helping tie every job or action to the overall goals and objectives?

5

THE THIRD PRINCIPLE: TEAM IS ALWAYS FIRST

> Team members must be collectively responsible for the team's
> success and understand everything that responsibility entails.
> —General Stanley McChrystal

Are Teams Still Relevant?

Jon Katzenbach and Douglas Smith wrote *The Wisdom of Teams* in 1993. They explained that teams have been around for hundreds of years. Teams have many virtues, and the benefits of teams have been widely extolled. They discovered that the potential impact of a team, as well as the collective impact of many teams, on the performance of large organizations is woefully underexploited, despite the rapidly growing recognition of what teams have to offer.[1]

Those words were written over twenty-four years ago, and we continue to make similar observations in our work at ACHEV. Leaders understand most of the obvious points about teams, but the discipline implied by a team structure and the more subtle implications of team strengths remain elusive to most.

As General McChrystal explained in his 2015 book *Team of Teams,* the complex, rapidly changing environment we live in today demands more of us than at any time in the past. Katzenbach and Smith explain that teams need to be focused on achieving results. Today, it has become an imperative that teams achieve results more efficiently and more rapidly, and demonstrate the capability to adapt to continual change.[2] Performing at such a level requires commitment and understanding well beyond what is normally found in the workplace.

Responsibility and Teamwork

The team and its performance must always be the first priority. Regardless of the context of endeavor, whether sports, business, government, or the military, it is the team that accomplishes the task through the coordinated support and effort of each member.

Most teams don't approach their performance potential—not because they are incapable, but because they lack the knowledge and commitment required to develop such a high standard of excellence. Each team member must hold himself or herself personally responsible for the performance of every other team member.

Before reading on, consider the depth of meaning implied by the prior statement.

Understanding of how to perform at the highest level is often obscured by ritualized approaches to routine tasks. This is especially true in the business world. In organizations characterized by top-down leadership, it's very easy to focus on the top of the to-do list, whether it be cost reduction, improved production time, reduction of errors, or increased sales numbers. When a team becomes focused on one thing, they lose sight of the many other parts of the job that can create long-term learning and productivity. Most leaders today are consumed by the urgent items on their to-do lists, rather than on the vital items that are so easily put aside for the moment and are ultimately forsaken. Gaining high performance requires the leader to focus on vital points.

Measuring Leadership Success

The Japanese have a term, *hoshin kanri*, which suggests the goals of the business must always satisfy the customer, bolster the long-term health of the company, improve company processes, and develop the employees. That sounds logical, simple, and straightforward.

However, as Dr. Jeffrey Liker explains in *Developing Lean Leaders at All Levels*, it is not so easy. Toyota has learned to accomplish this in a manner that surpasses most Western enterprises. Toyota believes that the only way you can sustain improving results year after year is to have repeatable, defined processes that are continually improved by the people running those processes.[3]

Toyota believes every job has four responsibilities:

1. Produce a product that satisfies the customer, including internal customers
2. Perform in a manner that builds the company
3. Find a way to do what you are doing better
4. Always reflect on how you can perform better and positively impact the team

If any one of these aspects do not occur during a project or task, the leadership score is zero. Leadership is viewed from a multiplicative perspective rather than an additive one (2 x 2 x 2 x 0 = 0 rather than 1 + 1 + 1 + 0 = 3).

Although they use different terminology, military elites have similar beliefs and practices, thus raising their standard of excellence well above other organizations. There is no trophy for second best or participation.

Performance at this level requires maximum effort, focused on the team. As John Wooden, the NCAA men's basketball record holder for most national championships (ten), including seven in a row (also a record), and eighty-eight consecutive games won (a team record), has said many times, "It takes ten hands to score a basket!"[4]

Check the Ego

High-performance teams believe in the highest standards and pledge a collective responsibility to that end. Each member accepts responsibility for a 100 percent effort. The team understands the need to become better each day and to look for and offer help to other members and the team as a whole. Not everyone functions well in a high-performance team atmosphere, because not everyone will "check the ego."

There is no place on a high-performing team for an outsize ego. Members of great teams are stars at what they do. They are self-confident but fully understand they could not accomplish what they do without the skill, knowledge, and effort of every other team member.

It is possible to be supremely self-confident yet not have an outsize personal ego. Ego is expressed in terms of team. Jocko Willink, in *Extreme Ownership,* provides an excellent description of how to emphasize team, extreme responsibility, and continuous improvement in a cocky SEAL team to ensure that egos are kept in check. Coauthor Leif Babin summed up how the SEAL teams could have improved their performance: "We should have given even greater ownership of planning and execution to the troops."[5]

Building high-performance teams requires a leader who understands how the required skills and trust are developed and evolve. It cannot be ordered by the leader. Rather, it emerges from within the team. The leader encourages this emergence through an environment that is supported by a well-designed plan, rigorous observation, positive feedback, and coaching. Over time, feedback loops among the team members grow into a web, resulting in loyalty to each other and the team. It is this bonding that builds trust through experience.

Trust

As we said previously, beliefs, commitment to continuous improvement, and trust do not just happen. Those characteristics evolve as team members experience candor in their interactions. This body of experience builds the bonds of trust.

Many people think of SEALs as superhuman. They are certainly in fine physical condition, but the purpose of SEAL training is not to develop superhumans. The purpose is to build super teams.[6] During their training, SEALs tackle very few tasks alone. The goal is not to build people who can follow exact orders, but to develop trust among peers so that they can adapt as a small group. In fact, SEAL, Ranger, and Special Forces training is designed so that it is impossible to survive by executing tasks individually. Individual performance is taken out of the lexicon on day one.[7]

For military elites, trust is built through shared hardship over a period of years. The challenge for business leaders is to build this same level of trust without the same level of hardship and in less time than years.

Truth Telling

Yes, truth telling is possible! After studying the causes of airplane crashes for years, the FAA determined that, in most cases, the problem was not the airplane, but the cockpit crew. Upon acceptance of this finding, they charged groups of social psychologists, sociologists, and other experts to find a workable solution for improving pilot training. In the end, the solution was called Crew Resource Management (CRM), or Charm School, as the pilots have come to call it. The focus of CRM is group dynamics, leadership, interpersonal communication, and decision-making. It trains junior pilots to speak more assertively and captains to be less forceful, turning vertical command-and-control relationships into flexible, multidirectional, communicative bonds.[8]

When the water landing of US Air flight 1549 by Captain "Sulley" Sullenberger was studied, it was determined by computer analysis that the accomplishment of the crew was nearly impossible and could not be duplicated. It was further determined that their technical training had been completely irrelevant to the solution they achieved. No procedure for low-altitude, dual-engine failure existed *anywhere* in the industry. It was their interactive adaptability that proved crucial: "Because of time constraints, they could not discuss every part of the decision process; therefore, they had to listen to and observe each other.... The captain and the first officer had to work almost intuitively in a close-knit fashion."[9] They were able to do this because they were trained to communicate candidly, they worked as a team with common goals, and they used well-understood practices. They were, in fact, a high-performance team.

When new members are introduced into a team with similar training and experience, trust more readily occurs. The more broadly such things happen in the larger organization, the more readily people are assimilated in various teams. A culture of excellence develops. This is a bottom-up evolution.

It would not be surprising if many readers are becoming skeptical. Skepticism in response to the idea of truth telling likely springs from many less-than-positive personal experiences. But, truth telling—or, as Jack Welch describes it, candor—is "the biggest dirty little secret in business."[10] The lack of truth telling in corporate America is pervasive. Welch sums up the problem succinctly: "What a huge problem it is. Lack of candor basically blocks smart ideas, fast action, and good people contributing all the stuff they've got. It's a killer."[11]

Smart ideas, fast action, and the contributions of good people encompass just about every factor of high-performing teams. High-performing teams check their egos so they are able to receive feedback, feedback they believe to be positive and truthful. *Honest feedback is the backbone of high performance.* There is no room for half truths, little white exaggerations, or withholding. High-performance teamwork is based upon absolute candor, all the time, from every team member.

Rich Communication

Dr. Alex "Sandy" Pentland, a professor at MIT and director of MIT's Human Dynamics Laboratory, describes great teams as having five characteristics:

1. Members talk and listen to each other in roughly equal measure.
2. Members face one another and gesture in lively conversation.
3. Members connect directly, not just through the team leader.
4. Members carry on back-channel conversations.
5. Members regularly explore for ideas outside the team and bring them back.[12]

Professor Pentland's research has revealed that individual reasoning and talent contribute far less than expected to team results. The most contributory factor to success is how the team communicates. He asserts that the best way to select team members is not by talent and personal accomplishment, but by communication style. Build the team around successful communication patterns.[13]

Key Elements

The first measure of great team communication is the energy exhibited in member exchanges. Pentland defines energy as the number of members and quality of the members' participation. "High energy" means many members actively participating. The best exchanges are face-to-face and animated. Tone and body language are major impactors on energy. Telephone or video conferencing, while not quite as good as face-to-face interaction, can also demonstrate energy. Media that convey the least energy are e-mail and text messaging.

The second element of great team communication is *engagement*. Engagement is an equal flow of listening and speaking on the part of each member. High-engagement teams gather ideas, suggestions, and questions put forward by all members.

Pentland's research indicates that one-third of the variation in results between teams can be attributed to team energy and engagement. These elements should be observed from three perspectives:

1. How team members contribute to the team as a whole
2. How team members communicate with one another
3. How team members communicate with other teams[14]

The third element is *exploration*. More than other teams, high-performance teams seek outside connections as sources of help and ideas. Time and energy are both finite resources. The ration of time spent in engagement versus exploration tends to oscillate as dictated by the level of innovation required by the organization.

Continuous Learning

Some teams manage to reach the pinnacle of performance only to begin a long fall from grace. At one moment, they are able to reach deep inside and give that maximum performance. For some, that is enough, and they live on those laurels for the remainder of their lives.

That is a great gift, if you get it. The fact is that today's competitive environment has a very short memory. It demands that we continue to achieve. For that to happen, each member of the team must continue to learn, contribute to team improvement, and ensure that no member is consistently the weakest link. Sooner or later, a persistent weak link will be the downfall of a team. When that happens, it must be recognized as a team loss and not the sole responsibility of that individual.

Long-term successful teams build continuous improvement into every statistical measure. Continuous improvement must be mandated, measured, and rewarded. Each team member must be prepared to immediately assume the duties and responsibilities of the supervisor, or at least be in training to do so. This mind-set ensures that there are competent leaders at every level. Yes, this places a serious burden on each and every leader.

As we stated at the outset of this chapter, most teams are not capable or prepared to become highly successful. They are simply not willing to make such a commitment. Any executive who says he or she just doesn't have the time or money to mentor teams does not understand the full responsibility of leadership. Such an executive is ensuring the organization will never achieve sustainable greatness.

Exercises for Reflection and Learning

- Ask the leadership team of your organization's last big effort to measure their success by the Toyota multiplicative method. Does the score match the results? Discuss how the organization measures leadership success and question if those measures are indicative of the best leadership.
- Consider the level of truth-telling in your organization. Will that level enhance or detract from Pentland's measures of great team communication?

6

THE FOURTH PRINCIPLE: LEADER/ FOLLOWER COMMITMENT

The person who cannot lead and will not follow invariably obstructs.
–Cortes J. Bicking

The Leader/Follower Concept

Evolutionary leadership theory suggests that groups with leaders fare better than groups without. Leadership and followership were as critical to the survival of prehistoric humans on the savannah as they are today.[1] Good leadership does make a difference. As organizations move through the twenty-first century, during which skill, knowledge, and efficiency are becoming increasingly more critical, the difference between good and great will likely determine survival or nonsurvival. Survival requires every edge possible.

Historically, there has been a social contract between leaders and followers. The leader set the direction and controlled the action. The followers were expected to go along in support. The benefit to the followers was the protection afforded by the group and a share of the spoils gained from collective success.

Organizationally speaking, a similar social contract exists today. However, the relationship and distinction between leader and follower has changed. Dr. Barbara Kellerman points out that the assumptions on which those ancient social contracts were based are being challenged.[2] While the benefit of having leadership remains little questioned, the nature of followership has changed significantly. In the past, leaders were privileged to have much deeper access to information and a broader view of the

53

situation. They knew more! The dispersion of information, the need for more highly specialized skills, and the evolution of the knowledge/skill-based team has changed the dynamics for elite teams.

Elite Teams and the New Dynamic

Because of their specialized skills and knowledge, team members—formerly viewed as followers—expect and are encouraged to participate in collective decision-making and actions. There are moments during the operational process when they are expected to assume leadership positions. This transition can be observed in military elites and championship sports teams. This morphing is not comprehensible from the perspective of mechanistic thought.

While one identified "leader" still tends to have overall operational responsibility, the leadership role may change person several times during an operational process. This change is dictated by the specific knowledge or skill needed to maximize team performance in that situation. Teams that function in this way are cognizant of the unique value each member brings to the overall capability. They also believe they could not accomplish a high level of performance without those specific skills. In this sense, each team member is an equal.

A Conscious Choice

When one seeks to become a member of an elite team, the decision must represent a conscious choice by both parties: the individual and the team. Very few if any elite teams will accept new members on the basis of "giving it a try." Commitment must be 100 percent from all members.

The Leader/Follower Contract

Membership in an elite or high-performance team represents a social contract. The elements of that contract are specific. In chapter 5, we thoroughly discussed the first element of the leader/follower commitment: the team must come first. Second, there must always be a shared commitment to excellence, congruent with the organizational vision. Third, when members ask the question, "Can I trust you?" the answer must be a resounding "Yes!" Fourth, members must have no doubt that each cares about the other. And last, there must be mutual respect for what each member brings to the team.

These five points comprise the leader/follower contract. Together, they define the expectations of each party in the relationship that is a high-performing team.

Selection to membership requires possession of certain skills or the bilateral promise to attain those skills. Most important is the candidate's ability to communicate and assimilate into the team culture and mind-set. While some may question this point, the MIT Human Dynamics Laboratory has empirically proven that the patterns of communication among team members, especially democratic listening, far outweigh individual intelligence, personality, and skill combined as predictors of team success.[3]

The Second Element—What Is the Level of Commitment to Excellence?

People in an organization want to know what is expected of them. Beyond the well-manufactured hype and corporate communication displayed on shiny brass plaques, people want to know the realities. Human beings will rise to the level of expectation they perceive to exist.

People develop their perceptions through observation and personal experience. They take great interest in and carefully observe the leader's personal commitment to excellence. Regardless of whether the task is mundane or of major significance, the leader's commitment to excellence will be scrutinized. In that context, every leader must accept the fact that she or he is onstage twenty-four hours per day, seven days a week.

The prolific leadership author John Maxwell has propounded the concept of "the Law of the Lid."[4] He infers that a team is limited by the skills and goals of the leader. When a leader's expectations are set low, as has been shown in the fields of education and sports coaching, individuals and teams tend to perform up to but rarely beyond those expectations. Psychological studies confirm that people can be limited by the expectations of their leaders or teachers.

Dr. Peter Senge addresses this same point directly in *The Fifth Discipline*, with a different conclusion. Senge suggests there are striking examples in which the intelligence of the team exceeded the intelligence of any individual member, most notably the leader.[5] This could easily be the case of a team characterized by a leader/follower relationship. In fact, the Law of the Lid occurs most frequently in teams lead by strong top-down authority—the old mechanistic perspective. Top-down leadership puts a cap on performance through excessive control.

It is likely that most readers have experienced or observed success that occurred in spite of a particular leader's skills. This result is enabled when the team's collective knowledge is allowed to come forth. High-performance leaders set high standards for themselves and then strive to exceed those expectations by allowing the collective genius of the team to emerge.

People are frequently surprised when they are encouraged to continually seek excellence by giving an endeavor all they have—and then to take one more step.

The great coach John Wooden exemplified this principle. Coach Wooden is famous for the fact he did not emphasize winning. What he did emphasize was the meeting of his expectation, which was that his players would give all they had all the time.[6] Allowed to expand to its utmost limits, such a team becomes improvisational. Like a great jazz group, they perform in their own rhythm and time, in a manner that can be incomparable. Such performances are not highly choreographed. Greatness emerges dynamically, through the interaction. The players are "in the zone."

The Third Element—Can I Trust You?

Psychologically healthy people know what trust feels like and will readily claim they know what it is. When pressed to define the phenomenon, however, most are stymied.

For the purpose of this discussion, let's agree that trust is a positive orientation between oneself and others involved in some sort of relationship. The premise is that one person will take the other's perspective into account when making a decision or taking an action and will not violate agreements, codes, or standards.[7] In order to fully appreciate the phenomenon of trust, one must first realize that trust is built on an element of risk for all parties involved. Trust is, in fact, a gamble.

Organizationally speaking, there are many layers of trust. The people who agree to work for an organization trust that they will be paid as promised, usually in arrears, for a specified period or assignment. They also trust that the benefits promised will be rendered when claimed. They trust safety measures will be in place, commensurate with the job and pay.

The employer in turn trusts that the people hired will come to work and perform as agreed. The employer trusts that employees will learn the job; perform to the level of excellence specified; and respect the values, standards, and codes set forth by the organization.

All of this represents a lot of trusting before the first act of the employment agreement takes place. We hope the reader concludes from the above description that trust is the glue that holds every organization together. Every leader needs to keep this fact in the forefront of his or her mind every second of the day.

When trust is breached, whether on the shop floor or in the executive suite, the organization moves into a state of decay. If that state is not recognized, the decay will spread. Allowed to spread long enough, it will create a destructive environment that will eventually bring the organization down.

The technique for rebuilding broken trust is straightforward:

1. Acknowledge the breach of trust.
2. Apologize.
3. Explain how it occurred.
4. Describe the process to be put in place to prevent a recurrence.
5. Ask for help and support.

When a new leader is introduced into a setting, rarely does he or she have the luxury of time. It certainly would be nice if those in ultimate authority would give a leader three to five years to build trusting relationships, but the reality is that such relationships are assumed on day one. It is assumed the leader is trustworthy, and the team is charged with respecting the position the leader holds. In the same manner, the leader must assume that the team is trustworthy, as a unit and as individuals.

For this contract to have any chance of success, the leader must make an "all-in" investment. The team and its members *must* be trusted until *proven* otherwise.

Building a "We Orientation"

Leaders face a critical dilemma with respect to trust. The psychological literature tells us, and most of us intuitively agree, that building trust requires a significant time investment by all parties. In this context, the reference is to physical time (hours, days, months, years).

But according to researchers Linda Weber and Allison Carter, there are other measures of time that are meaningful to this discussion. *Subjective time* involves two people experiencing portions of their lives together so that a *we orientation* can be built.[8] Note that subjective time does not have to occur in physical time. The sharing of similar experiences through dialogue when appropriate situations arise: remembering when one's first child was born, expressing how one felt when a close relative died, recounting the joy of one's child graduating from college, or recalling the feelings of making a major mistake. Self-disclosure, appropriately offered, can bridge years of physical time while building an immediate we orientation. A skilled leader can overcome the time issue in building trust by creating we-orientation bonds through the disclosure of past experiences and practices.

Like so many noble solutions found in books about leadership, application of the we-orientation technique can prove difficult. The leader must be sensitive to the right moment. A leader cannot just begin sharing intimate experiences without strong connective openings. Building subjective time and a we orientation requires the right opportunity.

The dilemma of time can be mitigated in other ways. A leader can create a process that works to shorten real time by demonstrating trustworthy actions.

Create a Formal Decision Process

Create a decision process the team approves and will support, and then pledge your absolute commitment to that process. A leader is often called upon to make decisions that may not be popular. A decision must be based upon what is right for the situation, taking into consideration the best interests of the team and the company's vision and values. The leader must be free to make decisions that may not be popular and still maintain a trusting environment. This is best accomplished by having an already published decision process that is challengeable.

Challenging the Decision

Some mechanistic thinkers might fervently argue that a leader's decision should never be challenged. When an organization is privileged enough to have leaders who are always proven right and never make mistakes, then those leaders have probably earned the right to never be challenged. Since there is no evidence that such leadership has ever existed, everyone has the right and should be encouraged to challenge leadership decisions in an appropriate manner.

Practicality suggests that a leader cannot be left open to continual questioning and discussion during operational periods. Nothing could ever get done. The right to challenge must be balanced against the need to accomplish the task. This would seem to create a conundrum—unless the guidelines for challenging a leadership decision are tightly defined.

The Process and the Challenge

A sound decision process must be transparent and provide for leadership accountability to the team. (See "Example of a Decision Process" figure shown on next page.) The team and/or any member must have the right to challenge any decision *based upon process*. The right to challenge a decision does not exist unless the process was not followed. This is an important point! A defective process is cause for review of the decision but does not automatically give rise to a reversal.

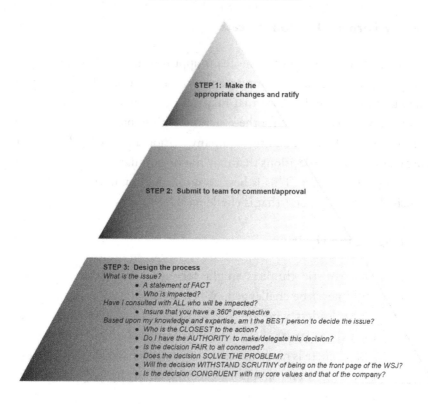

STEP 1: Make the appropriate changes and ratify

STEP 2: Submit to team for comment/approval

STEP 3: Design the process
What is the issue?
- A statement of FACT
- Who is impacted?
Have I consulted with ALL who will be impacted?
- Insure that you have a 360° perspective
Based upon my knowledge and expertise, am I the BEST person to decide the issue?
- Who is the CLOSEST to the action?
- Do I have the AUTHORITY to make/delegate this decision?
- Is the decision FAIR to all concerned?
- Does the decision SOLVE THE PROBLEM?
- Will the decision WITHSTAND SCRUTINY of being on the front page of the WSJ?
- Is the decision CONGRUENT with my core values and that of the company?

Jody learned the value of this technique soon after he was elected to the city council of his hometown. Every month, the city council met to discuss and vote on issues concerning the city.

His first vote concerned a highly controversial issue. After the vote, the good people of the city made him aware of their opinions by various means. According to the unofficial tally he kept beside his home phone, half the people liked his position, and the other half thought he should be hanged.

After a few more meetings, the council faced another high-profile, high-intensity vote. Once again, Jody was quickly made aware of the voters' feelings. Less than six months into his official tenure, it became obvious that he had antagonized about half the citizenry on the first vote and the other half on the second vote. A simple walk down Main Street became an act that required thorough consideration.

Lesson learned. A leader cannot expect to hold the respect of those he or she leads based upon popularity or an aggregate agreement with decisions made. There will be times when the decisions faced offer no popular choice, but the leader must make and hold true to the difficult choices.

Often, the answer that reflects the best direction for the long-term future of an organization will be unpopular with many, possibly the majority. But the leader has the responsibility for making those tough calls and standing behind them. A leader can only survive unpopular decisions if the people trust the wisdom and decision-making process employed by that leader. They must be made aware of how the leader makes decisions and believe that the process is fair, followed, and in the best long-term interest of the group as a whole.

Admit When You Are Wrong

Another important technique for building trust is to admit mistakes and take responsibility for bad decisions as soon as they come to light. Do not shift the blame! Take the hit, admit it openly, apologize, and tell the team what you will do to ensure the same mistake does not occur again. People understand that human beings make mistakes and will tend to forgive, but they will never forgive a lie or any attempt to cover up.

The steps for addressing mistakes are as follows:

1. Admit and take responsibility for the mistake as soon as it is discovered.
2. Apologize for any disruption the mistake has caused.
3. Disclose (within the legal and ethical boundaries) how the problem occurred.
4. Describe how the mistake will be remedied.
5. Describe what will be done to mitigate the problem and prevent it from recurring.
6. Apologize again!

The Fourth Element—Do You Care about Me?

"Me" is not an ID number, a job title, or a tool that is interchangeable and can be discarded based upon the head count or balance sheet. "Me" is a person with a history, family, hopes, dreams, fears, and needs. Each person is unique and responds to a given stimulus in a personal way. "Me" wants to know the level of respect that he or she can expect from the organization and its leaders.

It is this personal uniqueness that brings complexity to each and every organization and team. Leaders' and team members' empathy for these human interactions builds the foundation for trust and fosters engagement with the work, with teammates, and with the organization. Many studies have shown that such engagement is a critical factor in productivity and long-term employee retention. The creation of an environment in which the people feel cared for can have a direct impact on the profitability and survival of the organization.

Years of research conducted by the Gallup organization show that employee engagement has consistently operated at levels below 40 percent in most US corporations. Collectively speaking, we as a society remain unable or unwilling to make meaningful change.[9]

According to researcher and therapist John Selby, "Our society spends 15 to 20 years training the next generation to intellectually perform well at work, but devotes almost no time or training to the emotional dimensions of relating and success."[10] The uneasy truth is that most people in leadership positions do not know how to demonstrate genuine caring in a professional setting. Unfortunately, there are few high-profile leaders who are role models in this regard.

Nelson Mandela provides a wonderful contrast in the way he cared for and understood those he was entrusted to lead. Black South Africa saw him as their savior and the one who would vindicate all of their past suffering. He understood their plight and their hopes, but he rose to a higher plane of caring. He embraced many of the best customs of white South Africa, knowing that as a leader he must try to demonstrate caring for all if he was going to lead the entire nation to a greater future.

At the time, many felt he cared for his past oppressors more than he should. Mandela cared more than he was expected to or had to. Through such caring, he was able to bring a greatly divided nation together, at least while he was alive. As a person, he aspired to care enough to become a leader that *all* respected.

Dr. Martin Luther King Jr. observed, "In many neighborhoods and work places it has become every person for himself or herself. Caring takes a back seat to getting more and pushing harder, no matter what the cost."[11] Dr. King wrote those words in 1963, and they remain unsettlingly relevant today. The notable exceptions are in the hearts and minds of elite, high-performing teams. Those who have had the privilege of being part of a high-performing team realize that the "every man for himself" mind-set will destroy a team.

Caring That Much

The poets Samuel Coleridge and William Wordsworth offered great thoughts on how to start caring:

- Care more than you have to.
- Be slower to judge.
- Be quick to look deeper to sense the goodness in others.
- Engage in small, nameless, unremembered acts of kindness and love.[12]

A discussion about genuine caring is similar to a discussion about building trust. Caring is about personal interaction and requires time. The techniques are not difficult and only require observing, asking relevant questions, and reacting accordingly. Caring involves getting to know people on a personal level—learning about their values, families, problems, worries, hobbies, hopes, and dreams. (See appendix D, "Personal Values Exercise.")

A high-performance leader needs a diary in which to make notes every day concerning what has been learned about the people she or he serves. That information can be garnered informally, in passing, formally, socially—whenever possible. The mere act of gathering and recording these observations demonstrates more caring than most of those people will ever experience outside of their family life.

There is a pest control company in Birmingham, Alabama, whose leader provides a wonderful example of caring. The company is owned and operated by a certified public accountant who took it over when the original owner lost interest. Soon thereafter, this company began to grow, experiencing a high level of referrals and public recognition for quality work. This was somewhat unusual because the pest control business is not what anyone would consider a glamorous or high-growth industry.

When asked why the company was doing so well and why there was such loyalty to a pest control operation, the leader said nothing. He reached into the top drawer of his desk and pulled out a large, folded sheet of paper that had the complete organizational chart on it. Beside *each* name there was a specific Bible verse that applied to the particular needs of that person. Every morning at six o'clock, the leader came to the office, read each verse, and prayed for each of his people.

Regardless of one's spiritual inclination, the mere fact that a leader would spend so much mental effort on the needs of those for whom he was responsible sets a very high bar for caring.

The Fifth Element—Mutual Respect for What Each Brings to the Team

Diversity of thought is the leader's greatest tool. Over the span of a career, a leader will face many difficult decisions. Even the smallest of those decisions will have ramifications far beyond the leader's personal awareness. Given such an awesome responsibility, the leader must strive to gain insight and wisdom from every possible source. He or she must be acutely aware of not having all the best answers or commanding understanding of all things.

Leader and followers on all great teams deeply respect what each member brings to the situation. They realize that peak performance is only achieved when all are tasked with maximum input (effort and expressed thought). They innately understand that people wish to be heard and respected for what they can contribute.

Jack Welch fervently believes that every person in the world wants voice and dignity, and every person deserves them.[13] If there are people on the team or in the organization whose voices the leader does not respect, questions should be asked:

- How did they become part of the team in the first place?
- If they were once valued but no longer enjoy that respect, what happened?

- What has been done to remedy the problem?
- If the lack of respect still exists after remedial efforts, why do they still hold positions on the team?

Mutual respect is built through concerted effort to understand. If such respect does not exist, find a mirror and contemplate the problem and what it means to the viability of the organization.

Exercises for Reflection and Learning

Rarely in the historical study of organizational development or leadership can examples be found where the followers were asked how they would like to be led. Most often, those in power, usually the leaders, decide how they want to lead. Such decisions reflect the leaders' personal experience and possibly a modicum of study. In practice, the style of leadership mirrors what is comfortable and convenient for the leaders. What would the impact be if the experienced followers were asked to select leadership practices they preferred?

1. Share this book with a cross-section (executives, midlevel leaders, general workforce) of employees or team members.
2. Ask them to read each chapter. Pick two ideas from a chapter they feel, if practiced, would lead to higher performance.
3. Collect the findings and compare the differences in response from the various levels.
4. What does that information tell you? How will you respond?

7

THE FIFTH PRINCIPLE: CONTINUOUS IMPROVEMENT AS A WAY OF LIFE

> Unless you try to do something beyond what you have
> already done and mastered, you will never grow.
> –Ralph Waldo Emerson

Coach John Wooden often conveyed important lessons he learned from his father through sharing in subjective time. His father continually told him and his three brothers "not to worry about whether you are better than somebody else, but never cease trying to be the best you can be. You have control over that, but not the other."[1]

Continuous personal improvement is the hallmark of successful people. Wooden never emphasized winning, but rather giving 100 percent in an effort to be the best you can be. Embedded in his message is the belief in continuous improvement on the part of the individual for the betterment of the team.

Become the best you can be for a higher purpose than yourself. Members of continuous improvement cultures often display a similar set of beliefs. They tend to support challenging the status quo with respect to practices, methods, and thinking. Knowledge and understanding develop in the human mind in an emergent fashion. Humans build from observation and experience. If one accepts this premise, it follows that the state of "knowing" is temporary—there is always another piece to the puzzle. If that new piece is not sought and discovered, the enterprise loses competitive advantage in that area.

Challenge occurs in an environment that is highly collaborative. Individuals and teams work together, reflecting on their successes, failures, and ongoing actions. They discuss the thinking behind these actions in a nondefensive atmosphere. There is no place for blame, only shared personal responsibility for improvement. This is accomplished through strong efforts to build trust and respect, as we discussed in chapter 6.

The Learning Organization

Senge published *The Fifth Discipline* in 1990 and introduced the concept of the "learning organization" to the leadership discussion. "Team learning is vital because teams, not individuals, are the fundamental learning unit in modern organizations."[2]

A core paradox in today's leadership/management discussion is how to get an organization to learn and perform at the same time. The extreme case of performance-oriented thinking sees training time as wasteful, since it takes time away from productive work. Such leaders argue that a *lean* work environment does not allow enough time or money for organization-sponsored development of employees to the levels theorists suggest. Such thinking reminds me of a CFO who challenges, "If training is an investment, show me the return ratio I receive for the dollars I invest."

The mechanistic mind-set often knows very little about how to inquire into collective experience in ways that catalyze the emergence of new ideas, processes, and solutions by aligning with and amplifying the untapped wisdom in the organization.[3] A mature learning organization has experienced what Senge refers to as a shift of mind. From the organizational perspective, he means the people have changed their thinking from seeing problems as caused by someone or something "out there" to the recognition that their own actions have created the problems they are experiencing.[4] They collaborate to understand and change their processes and methods to achieve performance in ways they have never previously considered. Without a learning organization culture, any improvements will simply be events that are disconnected, sporadic, and random.

Dr. Bicking's research on *lean* implementation failure rates (rates of dissatisfaction or failure approach 90 percent) sheds some light on the surprising statistic. Since *lean* is supposedly based upon the foundational tenets of the Toyota Production System (TPS), his research examined a subject company that had attempted to implement *lean* several times over a period of years, achieving less than satisfactory results each time, and then compared the subject company with a Toyota division.

Every participant at the subject company and at the Toyota division responded to a stack-rank survey, which is ranking a series of statements in importance and relevance to their company. The stimulus statement that registered the widest response gap was *There is a strong effort to continuously challenge the status quo.* The Toyota division ranked this question first out of fifteen, while the subject company ranked it fourteenth out of fifteen. The intensity rank for Toyota was +6.25 (very strong) versus the subject company's -2.04 (relatively weak). The takeaway: learning is about constantly challenging the status quo and accepting full responsibility for needed change.[5]

The Disciplines of Continuous Improvement

Learning organizations are rarely victims of the external environment, because they fully accept responsibility for their current situation and finding the path to future success. According to Senge, achieving such a shift in mind requires five component disciplines. He described those disciplines as systems thinking, personal mastery, mental models, building shared vision, and team learning.[6] An organization seeking to maintain a continuous improvement environment employs each of these disciplines.

Systems Thinking

Senge uses the analogy of a rainstorm for a vivid explanation of systems thinking. Clouds mass, the smell in the air changes, skies darken, trees sway, leaves twist, and the first drops are felt. Puddles begin to appear and the process of runoff can be observed, feeding nearby streams and lakes. Conclusion announces it's coming with gentler breezes and blue skies. "All of these events take place over varying times and space, yet they are connected within the same pattern."[7] Each phase is connected and influences the rest, even though hidden from view at the particular time. The rainstorm can only be understood in its entirety (the whole), not by describing the phases as separate events.

Organizations, like rainstorms, are systems bound together by many factors that cannot always be seen. The problem of understanding any human system is further compounded when we are part of that same system. Our actions, even if the action is merely observation, can change outcomes. Systems thinking is a body of knowledge that helps in the clarification and understanding of how the system evolves. It is only through systems thinking that we become fully aware that an organization is continually evolving, even without leadership intervention; a point that every leader must be critically aware.

Personal Mastery

Personal mastery implies individual striving for a high level of skill. In this sense, personal mastery cannot be accomplished. It is an ongoing effort toward a constantly moving target. Like knowledge, mastery of any skill is fleeting, because new methods and information are continually being developed. For example, if one is an expert in networking technology and sets out to write a book about the newest implementations, the current pace of innovation would make the material old news before the book could be published. In order to remain cutting edge, a person must be in learning mode for his or her entire career.

People who consider themselves lifelong learners exhibit personal mastery. Like great athletes, they realize the attainment of one plateau only reveals a greater height to be scaled. Senge makes an important point: "An organization's commitment to and capacity for learning can be no greater than that of its members."[8] The Japanese culture offers an excellent example of how to create and practice such commitment. They call it *hansei*. The term does not easily translate, but implies individual reflection for the purpose of improving one's own performance in a manner that also improves the organization as a whole.[9]

In practice, most organizations do not seem capable of developing their people toward personal mastery. Therefore, those who do reach this level of thinking gain a distinct advantage.

Mental Modeling

The concept of mental modeling is corollary to the concept of shared vision. A mental model is the deeply ingrained set of values, assumptions, generalizations, and images that influences how members of an organization understand the environment in which it operates, and how internal actions are perceived to impact desired outcomes. The mental model becomes ingrained through continual reference to the vision concerning the congruence of all actions with that vision. As stated earlier, congruence can only occur if the vision is fully known (repeated verbatim), understood (applied to the required actions of every job position), and related to organizational measures of success.

Most readers are aware of examples in which team wisdom and performance far exceeds that of any individual on the team. It is a beautiful thing to be a part of such a team. A thirst is created to make it happen again and again. The experience creates a self-reinforcing, positive spiral, capable of propelling each member and the team to previously unrealized heights.

This spiral starts when the team begins to learn together. Learning together is rooted in open dialogue. Open dialogue is the capacity of a team to suspend assumptions and explore possibilities of improvement in every aspect of their performance. Everything is open for challenge and change.

The first rule concerning the suspension of assumptions is the removal of blame from all discussion. Whenever blame enters the dialogue, it brings with it the natural human need to assume a defensive position. People who are in a defensive mental mode are not capable of collaborating toward a positive end. Blame has no place in a learning organization. It takes up time and consumes valuable energy that should be used to solve problems and develop new and better ways.

Senge concludes his discussion of the five disciplines required of a learning organization with an admonition, "It is vital that the five disciplines develop as an ensemble."[10]

This point is brought home in every discussion concerning the extremely high historical failure rate in *lean* implementation efforts. Many companies have tried to implement *lean* and various aspects of TPS; most meet with failure, inability to sustain, or less than desired results.

Dr. Jeffrey Liker's observations concerning *lean* failures, in books like *The Toyota Way, The Toyota Way to Continuous Improvement*, and others, constitute an admonition to those seeking to create continuous improvement environments. Leaders cannot cherry-pick bits and pieces if they expect to achieve the full benefits of a certain model.

Each piece of Senge's five learning organization principles overlaps and supports the others. This is likewise true of TPS. It is a leadership mistake, if one seeks the full benefits of learning organization theory or TPS, to pick and choose only the appealing pieces of the puzzle and expect to finish with a complete picture.

Challenge the Status Quo

Status quo refers to the way things are. It can refer to the way things are at this very moment or, in the broader sense, how things are generally— how things have been in recent history, how those same things tend to be in the current daily routine, and how we expect things to be in the foreseeable future. From the organizational development perspective, the status quo encompasses habits, customs, processes, methods, culture, and all the assumptions that support the system.

A discussion of status quo is important to the topic of learning organizations for two reasons. First, as collections of human beings, we have a strong bias toward maintaining the status quo. We do not tend to like change; it makes us uncomfortable. Therefore, the status quo is easier to maintain. Maintaining avoids psychological trauma. Second, despite our efforts to keep things the same, change is constantly occurring in ways that are not always obvious or positive. (Does a status quo ever really exist?) Leaders must constantly be on the alert for subtle occurrences that can have a profound impact on the future.

The status quo of every organization is supported by a set of assumptions. Those assumptions can be publicly acknowledged and archived in traditions, or they can be unspoken. The leader must work hard to be fully aware of the supporting assumptions that undergird the status quo, and continually challenge their current validity. When assumptions are critically observed and questioned, it can be enlightening to discover the waste and problems that arise from them.

Reflection

Donald Schon wrote *The Reflective Practitioner*, originally aimed at professionals. Since its publication in 1983, it has been more frequently applied in the field of education. Schon redefined teachers as coaches, a point that should not be lost on all business and organizational leaders. He believed that optimal learning conditions are achieved when teaching ceases and reflective conversations begin.[11] Students (team members) are responsible for learning independently, through the guidance of a nurturing coach (the leader). The coach has the opportunity to become a co-learner, and much larger opportunities for learning become possible.[12]

The Japanese employ a term, *kaizen,* which means continuous improvement. For anyone who has ever participated in a *lean* project, the term is familiar. Unfortunately, the depth of the term is rarely understood in most *lean* endeavors. This lack of understanding centers around the practice of *hansei* (self-reflection) and is probably responsible for many failed *lean* attempts.

Although often overlooked in Western business, *hansei* is an essential element of *kaizen*. According to George Yamashina, head of the Toyota Technical Center, "Without *hansei* it is impossible to have *kaizen*."[13] Before anyone can begin to practice *hansei* correctly, there is an essential first step: the acknowledgement that every individual has shortcomings, and that it is the responsibility of the individual and the team, together, to recognize these shortcomings and to help in overcoming them. In so doing, the entire team raises its capability through understanding.

The concept of *hansei* is foreign to most Western thinking. The Japanese teach this concept early in childhood for the purpose of encouraging self-improvement. They see self-improvement as a group activity. They have also found that self-improvement efforts work best when there is constant encouragement and help from classmates.[14] Students do not learn it from specific instruction, but from ongoing experience.

No such concept is taught in Western schools, except in the case of certain Jesuit schools. But the concept, how it is learned, and the result are very reminiscent of the concept of esprit de corps (the spirit of the team/unit) that prevails in some high-performing sports teams and every elite military unit (Rangers, Special Forces, SEALS). As these examples imply, having esprit de corps is an indication of potential for superior performance. In fact, for such teams, reflective collaboration is the precursor for superior performance. Open and honest sharing among team members is an essential for high performance. It is an art that requires effort and constant practice, and should be considered a prerequisite for leadership.

Journaling as a Tool for Reflection and Learning

The practice of journaling is an effective tool for a leader seeking to become more proficient at self-reflection. The simple act of taking a small amount of time at the end of one's day to look back and critically review the day's particular actions is therapeutic and instructive. Entries are short comments concerning actions taken during the day. Points should include

- the action taken,
- the results of the action,
- how the action was received, and
- ideas on what could have been done differently.

There is no magic in any one day's comments, but the patterns and the interconnectedness of a month's set of comments usually provide important insights into the way an individual handles situations. Over several months, one can connect leadership actions to actual outcomes, both positive and negative. Patterns emerge that offer revealing tendencies and opportunities for improvement.

The spirit of continuous improvement always begins with self. John Wooden exhorted his teams to deliver a 100 percent personal effort, whether in practice or a game. In Wooden's eyes, you were a winner if you gave all you had, regardless of what the scoreboard said.[15] If we compare ourselves against another entity, then we are limiting our potential. The continuous improvement questions are easy:

- Is this the best we can do?
- Is there something more we could have done?
- Is there something we could have done differently?
- Are there assumptions we are making that hold us back?

No team can be kept from the winner's circle if every player strives to give their very best and continually helps the other team members to reach the pinnacle of their ability.

Never stop learning! Challenge the status quo everywhere you encounter it. Challenge with an open mind and without blame. Never stop reflecting on what is possible.

Good, better, best—if you never let it rest, you will eventually become the best.

Exercises for Reflection and Learning

Begin a personal leadership journal.
Team Continuous Improvement Exercise

1. Schedule a team meeting. Ask the team to collaboratively explore the four continuous improvement questions:
   - Is this the best we can do?
   - Is there something more we could have done?
   - Is there something we could have done differently?
   - Are there assumptions we are making that hold us back?
2. Make the answers exhaustive; nothing is too trivial for consideration.
3. When the lists are complete, challenge the team to create countermeasures for each item.
4. Analyze the list of countermeasures for viability and multiple impacts.
5. Prioritize the actions and establish time frames for review, reflection, and revision.

8

THE SIXTH PRINCIPLE: DELEGATION—SHORT-TERM FOCUS FOR LONG-TERM SUCCESS

> The ability to delegate is the single most essential
> leadership skill for organizational growth and for
> maximizing the productivity of any professional.
> –Roger C. Allred

The military uses starburst munitions to flood the battlefield with light, making the obscure more visible. The art world describes a starburst as an explosion of light or color, with rays emanating from a central point. Today's leaders need to think about the starburst effect of delegation as a tool for illuminating organizational purpose and highlighting what might be obscure knowledge or awareness. In doing so, they will lay the foundation for the possibility of exponential growth in learning, productivity, and development.

While experts proclaim that delegation is an essential leadership skill, experience indicates significant mistaken assumptions exist concerning the practical application. It is widely assumed that the act of delegation is fully understood. Often, however, delegation is used simply to refer to the assignment of a task. Less often, delegation reflects a well-thought-out process directed at aiding the learning and growth of individuals within the organization.

The military elites practice delegation from the deeper perspective. The reason for this should be obvious; at any given moment during an operation, the military leader might be permanently removed from the battlefield, leaving the unit leaderless and less effective. Well-trained military units practice for this possibility, preparing the team for transition when it occurs in reality.

Such preparation facilitates hands-on, real-life learning and growth. In the military, a leader's first responsibility is to ensure the training and competency of his or her immediate replacement. The effective leader finds a way to connect every task with some level of learning. Organizations practicing delegation from a growth orientation will not be rendered or slowed by ineffective unexpected change in leadership. More importantly, such organizations will continually learn and improve.

Delegation Defined

Delegation occurs when a person with authority gives that authority to someone else to act on his or her behalf. Such a definition suggests a broader concept than simply directing an employee to carry out an assignment.

Delegation—A View from the Top

Many large organizations put a lot of time, effort, and planning into the development of senior executives. In that context, the process is not usually described as delegation. In actuality, executive development is delegation aimed at a select group of senior individuals. The process involves training, a designed program that includes developmental assignments, and periodic review of progress and readiness for the next level of responsibility. Executive development always includes the passing of authority along with accountability.

Most human resources experts agree that executive development programs and personal coaching are effective. One dilemma always arises: which people from what level should be eligible for selection? The answer will be different for each organization, but the factors considered tend to be consistent from one organization to another:

- budget constraints
- time constraints and scheduling
- location of available space
- identification of appropriate subject matter

Balancing resource availability with the benefits of developing people will always be challenging.

Delegation—A View from the Bottom

Most people think of delegation as some variation of a six- or seven-step process learned in a basic business course and directed toward lower-level employees. The image invoked tends to be an outgrowth of Taylor's mechanistic thought. The manager simply pushes the button (starts the delegation process) and voilà, the job is executed—a mere matter of following prescribed steps. Unfortunately, as in most mechanistic processes, the end result rarely matches the theoretical expectation.

Delegation involves people, and as discussed previously, people add complexity and variation. Just like executive development, effective delegation requires thought, planning, and dedication from the responsible leader. A well-planned delegation assignment can produce expected or even better than expected results.

Employees completing a well-planned delegation assignment garner several benefits. They accomplish the relevant task, add to their current skill and level of confidence, and multiply the ability of the team to get more done. The delegation process also creates leverage for the leader, allowing more time for getting other tasks accomplished.

Mindful leaders continually strive to demonstrate a clear link between the delegated activity and the stated vision of the organization. In other words, the activity is framed as additive to the overall team effort. Team members want the delegated task to increase their skill level and understanding with respect to their current job track. They want any training or developmental task to directly increase performance.

Good people desire honest, positive feedback connected with some manner of modeling they can copy. Coaching and feedback should be individually tailored rather than generalized. (Remember the TODAY acronym method of recognition described in chapter 4.) The delivery and effective implementation of an important delegated project requires the focused attention of the individual leader.

An important module of every leadership engagement and alignment process (LEAP) delivered by ACHEV is the creation of personal development plans. In that two-hour segment, each participant begins the creation of her or his own career development plan, including goals, values, aptitudes, needs, and perceptions, along with time-specific action plan. (See appendix C, "GAPS Coaching.")

Participants quickly discover the assignment cannot be accomplished in two hours. The module concludes with the assertion that, upon returning to the workplace, each participant should conduct this same exercise with his or her direct supervisor and direct reports. After two and a half days of intensive training, that moment brings the participants face-to-face with reality—accepting a leadership role entails a major commitment to the success of others.

Reasons (Excuses?): Why Leaders Choose Not to Delegate

Leaders should use delegation regularly. Unfortunately, this is often not the case. Excuses for this lack of action abound. Here are samples:

- There are not enough hours in the day to delegate.
- I can do the task better than anyone else.
- I enjoy doing this task.
- My people are not capable.
- The staff is too busy to take on more work.
- If I delegate too much, my job could be threatened.
- Delegating may make my boss think I am lazy.
- Delegating tasks could cause me to lose control of the business.
- My employees will complain if I give them more to do.
- My employees don't have all the information at hand to make decisions.
- Getting more things done gives me the high profile I need to get promoted.

Sound familiar?

The Starburst Delegation Plan

The leader should consistently seek meaningful delegation opportunities. The planning may become intricate and should be in concert with individual developmental needs. When an opportunity is identified, the delegation process commences. Here is how to build a six-step developmental delegation plan:

- Step 1: Identify and define the task.
- Step 2: Match the appropriate person to the task.
- Step 3: Conduct the delegation plan meeting.
- Step 4: Seek acceptance and engagement.
- Step 5: Implement the development plan.
- Step 6: Follow up.

Step 1: Identify and Define the Task

When defining a task, the level of clarity and detail will vary according to circumstances, but needs to be sufficient so that no question exists on the part of the person being charged with authority. Any gap in information will be the cause of later need for explanation and/or suboptimal execution. Time spent by the leader on this step is well spent and saves future time. Questions that should be answered in the definition phase include:

- How does the task relate to the mission of the team and to the vision of the larger organization?
- What interconnective bridges will possibly be crossed during the execution, and are there any delicate issues that should be identified?
- What are the time parameters of the task?
- What are the communication expectations for the duration of the delegation assignment?
- What, if any, boundaries exist, and what level of autonomy and authority will govern the assignment?

Complete understanding of the task provides a clear connection to the larger organization and how other sections or team members are impacted by the assignment. Consider that any task can be perceived from varying perspectives. A first discussion with the selected team member might focus on familiarity and learning the process of the task at hand.

Later, that same task may be used to introduce the concept of continuous improvement. Ask the person to perform each step with the idea of discerning a better way of doing it.

Step 2: Match the Appropriate Person to the Task

When delegation is viewed from a development standpoint, more reflective time is required of the leader. The question rises above the basic considerations of who can do the job the best, quickest, or with the least oversight. In fact, from a development perspective, the best choice may be the slowest, the least experienced, or one who requires personal oversight.

It wouldn't be surprising if bells, whistles, and other alarms are going off in the reader's mind. We do understand the potential for frustration.

This is an excellent time to review some very important points. First, a leader has two and only two fundamental responsibilities: accomplish the assigned task and develop the members of the team. In doing so, a leader must always evaluate the use of his or her time from the long-term viewpoint.

In other words, will an extra hour spent here save five, ten, or more hours in the future? Spending the *right* time can actually save far more time. Leadership time spent aiding team development offers several other benefits, such as building trust, loyalty, confidence, and awareness of capability, both for the leader and the team member.

Questions that should become clear in the selection stage include the following:

- What are the needs of the individual?
- What level of coaching will be required?
- What is the availability of that coaching?
- What other support issues need to be addressed?
- What pertinent time factors are associated with this task?

When tasks are viewed from a developmental perspective rather than just a task to be done, every phase offers multiple opportunities, especially within a continuous improvement environment.

Step 3: Conduct the Delegation Plan Meeting

Developmental programs normally achieve higher levels of engagement when participants are allowed to be part of the design process. Granted, they may not be knowledgeable in the facets of the task, but their input and response to the leader's questions and comments can add value to the experience.

Begin the discussion with a clear description of the purpose and expectations. Using the points outlined in step 1, tie the purpose and expectations to the team mission and organizational vision.

Provide a timeline of progress and completion. Specifically explain the learning points attached to each action. Don't assume participants will make the connection between the learning points and the actions. While such connections may seem obvious to an experienced practitioner, that is not always the case for a learner. Make learning easy.

Describe the learning process and how the leader, supervisors, and mentors will provide assistance (demonstration, observation, critique). Explain what should be done if there are questions or difficulties. Provide the background, achievements, and experience of the mentors. If possible, introduce the teachers and other supporting persons.

Ensure participants are fully aware of how they will be judged and the type and amount of feedback they should expect. Provide them with specific methods of communication and schedules for interface with their immediate leader.

Always remember that quality training and development is appreciated. It is an excellent means of building a relationship of trust.

While the leader remains constantly responsible for the training and development of those under her or his supervision, this does not mean the leader must always be the deliverer of that training. Regardless, he or she should work hard to stay in contact as the task proceeds.

In keeping faith with that belief, the leader should ensure the person being trained sees all fitness reports associated with the development process. Never leave room for surprises. The initial plan, activity descriptions, feedback, communication, and reports should be memorialized for future reference and continuous improvement study.

At the end of this formally scheduled meeting, seek out any questions that might exist. Clarify understanding and, most importantly, ask participants if they feel fully capable of successfully completing the task and acquiring the learning objectives. Any doubt should be cleared up before the conclusion of the meeting.

Step 4: Seek Acceptance and Engagement

Whenever the organization offers to provide a developmental opportunity, there should be a corresponding commitment by the recipient. The leader should expect from the person to whom the task is delegated a firm commitment to put forth best effort.

Suggest that a learning log be maintained. This a written report of the training, comments on the quality of the learning experience, and any suggestions as to how the individual could have done more (a reflective exercise to improve their personal learning capability), and how the process could be improved. This may sound excessive, but it is this type of exercise that fosters a learning organization environment.

Step 5: Implement the Development Plan

Regardless of the time required for the task, the leader must remain conscious of the purpose and progress of activity. The engaged leader will make frequent contact, assuming she or he is not directly involved in the teaching process. Inquire about the engagement of the learner and offer encouragement. Offer suggestions aimed at enhancing the experience. As anyone who has ever sat through lectures recalls, it is easy to lose focus. A brief phone call or conversation from the leader to check in can help overcome such moments and remind the student of the importance of the opportunity.

Step 6: Follow Up

Set a time for discussing the entire process. Inquire about the validity of the initial plan and the learning objectives. Make every effort to discover if the learning objectives were achieved, and *celebrate* success. Review the important points and seek out problems or issues that could be improved.

Encourage the discussion of solutions, and share those findings with the appropriate people. Ask the participant about changes he or she would make to improve the personal learning experience. Incorporate those changes into the next developmental task. Be certain to ask the person how you, as the leader, could have improved your assignment and oversight of the delegation task.

Exercises for Reflection and Learning

1. Have you planned and executed a delegation assignment in the past sixty days? If not, why not? If yes, reflect on the delegation process and the result achieved. How did your planning and overall process square with the steps outlined in this chapter?

2. Identify at least two delegation opportunities that exist within your operation. Use the delegation process outlined in this chapter and execute these opportunities. Be sure to complete a postaction review to determine what went well and how you could have improved the process.

SECTION 3

Over our many years of leadership experience, postgraduate education, and coaching, we have been exposed to many different leadership situations. The causes of situations were as numerous and varied as the situations themselves. However, we have come to the conclusion that every problem we have witnessed could have been avoided, shortened, or solved if the leaders involved had possessed two basic skills.

Section 3 contains three chapters. Chapter 9 discusses the art of conflict management, emphasizing that conflict can be a highly proactive tool for innovation and problem solving. A method for managing potentially destructive conflict is provided, as well as a procedure for using proactive conflict as a method for constructive innovation.

Chapter 10 addresses the important skills of listening and asking good questions. Leaders today spend far too much of their time telling and giving instruction, rather than listening and learning.

The last chapter describes a real consulting engagement, using the mind-sets and principles we have presented throughout this book. The results discussed were the actual results achieved, and provide a view of the potential that can be created commitment to apply the knowledge set forth in *The Leadership Drought*.

9

THE TWO-EDGED SWORD—CONFLICT

The people to fear are not those who disagree with you, but those
who disagree with you and are too cowardly to let you know.
–Napoleon Bonaparte

While striving to build the best teams and organizations possible, leaders will find themselves in social interactions of various types, each encompassing some level of conflict. Effective leaders must be prepared to manage conflict in its various forms. Managing conflict is one of the true litmus tests of leadership. Successful conflict management requires an understanding of the different categories of conflict.

To best understand the concept of conflict, it is helpful to begin with the end result. Generally speaking, conflict situations result in either constructive outcomes or destructive outcomes; rarely will any conflict situation leave an organization unaltered. Recall the discussions in chapter 2 concerning complex adaptive systems (CAS). The change in attitude or action of one individual can potentially alter the sequence of events throughout the entire organization. Conflict, in whatever context, is the ultimate representation of that potential.

The overarching theme presented in this book is the creation of a culture that strives for continuous improvement leading to the realization of a positive shared vision. Therefore, we have attempted to focus on the potential constructive outcomes of conflict, while also addressing the real dangers of destructive outcomes.

All conflict can be sorted into one of three categories. Two categories offer constructive potential. The third category, interpersonal conflict, has the destructive capacity to bring down any organization. It is also omnipresent, requiring the constant vigilance of the entire leadership team.

- *Conflict of ideas* refers to contrasting thoughts about a problem, opportunity, strategy, or any conceptual issue. In chapter 7, we introduced the principle of continuous improvement as a way of life. Effective leaders embrace conflict for the purpose of generating ideas for improving the organization. This reflects conflict in a proactive sense. The leader initiates the conflict situation for positive outcome.

- *Conflict of coordination* refers to differing views about how to get work done, availability of resources for a project, responsibility for specific tasks, and so on. As in a conflict of ideas, the leader takes a proactive stance, initiating or encouraging ongoing dialogue concerning the status quo. The leader asks every team member to take a critical look at the underlying assumptions of every process and policy, seeking to create greater efficiency.

- *Conflict of people* refers to disagreements between two or more people. This type of conflict usually finds the leader in a reactive mode that can result in either gain or loss of trust, respect, and admiration, based on how quickly and effectively the problem is resolved. Interpersonal conflict is a natural by-product of all social interaction and therefore cannot be eradicated. Great teams and organizations learn how to effectively manage this ever-present reality of life.

Conflict of Ideas and Conflict of Coordination

Most people see conflict as disruptive. It is important to understand that conflict can be constructive and positive if well managed. In such cases, the leader takes initiative in the creation of a conflict situation. This is done to advance organizational performance through collaborative action. Developing creative and innovative solutions to complex problems requires an ability to access all relevant and even marginally relevant information for active manipulation.[1] According to Dr. David Sousa, an expert in cognitive neuroscience, participation in such an exercise requires significant mental resources and energy, and can be very tiring.

Some US presidents have used this approach as a leadership tool. Presidents including Abraham Lincoln, George Washington, Ronald

Reagan, and Franklin D. Roosevelt intentionally surrounded themselves with highly accomplished, strong-minded advisers and used vigorous debate among them to generate fully considered options concerning the problems of the day. These presidents had the vision to see that conflict could bring about a host of positive results.[2]

General Washington employed such a process during the Revolutionary War. Realizing he was facing a vastly superior force, Washington knew that he could not follow the currently accepted methods and rules of combat. To adapt to his situation, he devised a new form of war council. Instead of handing down battlefield assignments, he heard out impassioned arguments over strategy and tactics among officers of diverse backgrounds and inclinations. Washington listened and asked probing questions. When he made his eventual decision, everyone understood why, and knew that the decision took full account of the risks and uncertainties that their deliberations had revealed.[3] Washington's management of conflict enabled the upstart Continental Army to defeat a highly superior force.

As this example demonstrates, the energy that can be derived from conflict has the potential to create innovation—new perspectives, ideas, and actions that can positively impact organizational performance. This potential can be realized if the leader is prepared to engage in and facilitate the dynamics of an environment in which the status quo is challenged, healthy debate is encouraged, and everyone becomes engaged in the process of determining the best solution for the issue at hand.

US presidents who came to office during the Cold War embraced a new term for conflict between nations with significantly different philosophical perspectives. The term *constructive dialogue* emphasized the need to engage in communication for a positive future rather than arguing dogma. Discussion of the political and cognitive social science theories that supported this approach are beyond the scope of this book. But the positive impact of the constructive dialogue concept in the geopolitical context cannot be denied.

Few individuals and organizations seem to recognize that their primary value is in their collective knowledge. One person may have information that another does not have; parties have completely different sets of information. Or it may be that two groups have the same information but completely opposite perceptions of its significance. Regardless of the case, deeper understanding of information can only be additive to the quality of decisions made. Collective knowledge creates leverage that can be applied for the organization's benefit and the individuals' growth.[4]

Leaders must become adept at drawing upon the knowledge and wisdom that each team member possesses. Leaders must facilitate discussions that will dissect, debate, and ultimately overcome any problem. Changes in organizations never occur without such debate. The higher the skill level of leaders, the better the quality of change.

The ability to get successful results from situations of conflict can often be the literal difference between success and failure in an organizational setting. Whether a conflict arises organically or intentionally, the leader must have the skill to adroitly manage the circumstance.

A Strategy for More Creative Solutions

Michael Arrigo, an associate professor at Bowling Green State University, has some definite ideas about how a team can improve its creative outlook:

1. *List the attributes of the problem.* The list should be thorough so as not to miss any possible insight. Study the list and see if they, collectively, offer any new thoughts.
2. *List all the things you do not like about the problem.*
3. *Amplify the problem.* Instead of trying to solve the problem, think of all the things that could make the problem worse.
4. *Question your assumptions.* Review the problem and decide which assumptions are worth questioning and which battles are not worth fighting.
5. *Change your perspective.* The environment in which you work influences your thinking. Different environments trigger new thought patterns.
6. *Assume you are wrong.* Test your own solutions and reconsider possible solutions. This process encourages the team to look for variations and possible compromises.[5]

Conflict of People

The most common conflict encountered in the workplace is a conflict of people. Many factors can initiate such conflict, and the depth of conflict can range from simple to complex. In putting a plan together, there are some guidelines leaders should consider.

First, should the leader get involved? Time is a precious commodity for a leader. Becoming involved in an interpersonal conflict requires a significant commitment of time, along with the discipline to adhere to an already established process. Leaders should only get involved in conflict between persons when actually required—when there is no other alternative. To determine whether or not to get involved, answer three questions:

- Have the parties tried to work the problem out between themselves?
- Are the parties interdependent with respect to the team and its work?
- Is the conflict impacting the team?

People love to lay their problems on the desk of the leader. In doing so, they have unburdened their minds, but more importantly, they can feel they have off-loaded responsibility, giving them the freedom to walk away with no further consequence. This is a trap new leaders can easily become ensnared by. In an effort to demonstrate skill, knowledge, and worth, the new leader happily accepts the problem. Upon doing so, the leader then owns it.

The leader should only accept problems involving interpersonal conflict if the answers to the three questions above all result in a definite yes. If the parties have not worked to resolve the problem among themselves, the leader should remand it back to those involved, with a caveat: "If you are unable to solve it yourselves, then come back to me together. I will solve the problem, with the understanding that neither party may like my resolution." Create an environment in which it is in their best interest to solve such problems on their own.

Interdependence implies that each party relies, in some measure, on the other party to get their job done. If two parties have a personal issue, but have no connective work relationship, the matter is private and does not require intervention of the leader. The problem may impact one party's performance, and if so, that should be dealt with as a performance issue, but it does not merit conflict intervention by that leader. An excellent case in point would be when a member of the team becomes embroiled in a divorce proceeding. The leader should take great care in not becoming involved in the divorce itself.

Do the actions that stem from the interpersonal conflict impact the team's performance? If yes, the leader must get involved as soon as the problem is recognized. Failing to do so can quickly diminish the respect given the leader. Ultimately, this could result in loss of trust and respect for the larger organization.

The Interpersonal Intervention/Mediation Process

There are only three ways to resolve a conflict: power contests, rights contests, and interest reconciliation. People are biologically ill-prepared to resolve conflicts. They tend to react with flight (walking away or distancing from the problem) or fight (coercion or power plays). But we can learn to think our way out of conflicts. Dr. Dan Dana, a recognized expert in mediation and conflict reconciliation, provides a four-step method:[6]

Step 1: Find Time to Talk

- Meet with each party separately. Discover each party's point of view.
- Suggest a time and location for all parties to meet. Establish time parameters for planning purposes. The location should be neutral so that no party feels disadvantaged.
- Establish cardinal rules:
  - There will be no walking away.
  - There will be no interruptions.
  - There will be no power plays.
- State the expectation for successful resolution.

Step 2: Plan the Context

- Work to ensure there are no interruptions during the meeting. There can be no incoming phone calls or disruptions.
- Define exactly who will be in attendance.
- Ensure complete confidentiality.
- Choose a setting that is conducive to comfort and ease of dialogue.
- Outline the sequence of discussion.

Step 3: Talk It Out

- Express appreciation in advance for following the guidelines.
- Express optimism that the conflict will be resolved fairly and, as much as possible, to the satisfaction of all parties.
- Allow one party to begin while the other party listens.
- Stay in the essential process of respectful discussion and listening.
- Try to move from each party's original frame to reframe positions through increased understanding.
- Reward any conciliatory gestures by requiring the other party to offer an equivalent conciliatory gesture.
- Stay with the process until a breakthrough.
- Seek to move from "me against you" to "us against the problem."

Step 4: Make a Deal

- Specify the agreed upon future behaviors.
- Write it down. Make the results a permanent record that can be revisited, with ramifications should the problem once again arise.

Exercises for Reflection and Learning

1. Review a recent workplace conflict that you were involved with. How did your process for addressing the situation work? Did you have an actual plan or did you just wing it and hope for the best? What could you have done differently to improve the outcome?

2. Plan and initiate a positive conflict. Keep copious notes about the entire process. What worked and what didn't? Evaluate how you handled your role as a facilitator. What could you have done differently to improve the outcome?

10

LESS TELLING AND MORE ASKING
IMPROVE LISTENING

All of my experience has taught me that what builds a relationship, what solves problems, what moves things forward is asking the right questions.
        –Edgar Schein

Effective communication is essential in a healthy organization. Our actions, though, are often counter to this belief. For the most part, we go through life simply telling others what we think they need to know. Telling, as a first action, usually results in one-way communication rather than dialogue. It tends to shut the other side down. Then later, when some issue arises from what we thought was a simple instruction, we wonder why.

Generating bold new ideas, avoiding disastrous mistakes, and developing agility and flexibility require that we practice what Edgar Schein called *humble inquiry*. Schein defined humble inquiry as the art of drawing someone out by asking questions that you do not always know the answers to. It is building relationships based upon curiosity and interest in the other person or situation.[1]

Dr. Schein was an industrial psychologist who was fascinated by how much well-intended help is disregarded and even resented. He spent most of his time and research on learning how to offer, give, and receive help in a manner that is appreciated and respected, rather than resented. His books became popular around 2009, when *Helping* was first published.

This chapter offers practical support in building the leader/follower continuum. The work of Dr. Schein provides the basic rationale for our ideas. Every leader should read Schein's work (especially *Helping*, 2009, and *Humble Inquiry*, 2013).

In chapter 5, we discussed the concepts of trust and caring as important aspects of leadership. Listening was identified as a key skill, required to build trust and demonstrate a caring attitude. As leaders, we are constantly trying to help people overcome problems and perform better in various aspects of their lives.

Sometimes, however, our best intentions to help are not well received. Such efforts get described as micromanaging, know-it-all, overbearing, or sticking one's nose where it doesn't belong. The result leaves everyone in a state of resentment. Leaders can mistakenly judge those they tried to help as ungrateful or unwilling to learn.

All of us need to learn how to give and receive help if we are to tap into the full knowledge and wisdom existing in our teams. Schein suggests three things we can do that will help overcome the problems described above and become better collaborators and leaders.

- Do less telling.
- Learn to do more asking.
- Become better at listening.[2]

The Messages of Telling

Acts of telling can convey many messages to the receiver. When thinking about message, a leader needs to consider more than the words spoken. The collection of words may convey the intended message. That same collection of words may convey an unintended message. Additionally, the communication can wrap the receiver in a blanket of ideas and feelings that the sender may or may not have intended.

Often, a message sent centers around deficiencies or problems. When we embark on the problem-solving process, messages tend to be negative: what didn't happen, what happened that shouldn't have happened, and what went wrong. All such discussions focus on the negative aspects of a situation, drowning out any thoughts of what might have been done well or right.

Sometimes the message can be simple and straightforward, and other times the message can be complex, raising unspoken questions about meaning and emotion, and creating a lack of understanding that can produce significant problems.

This point cannot be overstated: regardless of intent, a leader's comments can have destructive capability well beyond what we normally imagine. Donald Trump has provided the quintessential example in his run for the presidency. A leader's words can explode, sending deadly fragments flying through the air. Words change the course of thought and action through misunderstanding and destroy relationships through misperception.

That may seem like an exaggeration of the danger involved every time a leader makes a statement, but it cannot be truer in the realities of social dynamics. We hope that every reader realizes the importance of thinking before speaking. Every one of us will become more aware of this reality as we journey through life. We will each fall prey to this danger many times. The key is to find ways of holding awareness high and mitigating the odds of unintended consequences as we communicate.

As you contemplate the navigational possibilities for surviving this communication minefield, ask yourself this: which type of statement has a greater chance of being misunderstood, a telling statement or a question?

We all do a lot of telling during a day. On the surface, it is socially acceptable and appropriate. Telling or directing certainly has an important place in the social dynamics of leadership and teamwork. When we engage in telling, we are communicating the following:

- I understand the situation completely. I am aware of your level of experience and involvement, along with your perspective. I am also aware of the complete sequence of events leading to this point.
- Based upon my knowledge and experience, I have all the answers concerning this situation.
- Because of my knowledge and experience, I know exactly what to do to remedy this situation.
- Because of my knowledge, experience, and awareness of all the possible options, I know the best way to do this.

We suggest the space in which all these points are true is narrow. Telling should be used with forethought and care. Telling is most appropriate in emergency situations. In an emergency, people must be made aware of a danger that they may not realize, and understand time is of the essence. There is no time for questions or indecision; action must be taken immediately.

Schein warns that telling can put the other person down. It implies the other person does not know what I am about to tell them.[3] Schein's warning speaks to the dangers of a situation in which the person is aware of what the leader is telling. It also clearly accentuates another situation in which telling is appropriate: when the receiver does not have knowledge about the point under discussion.

These two examples define the effective use of telling. A leader's ability to discipline her or himself in the use of telling can have a profound effect on that leader's relationship with the team and how the team reacts to cumulative daily exchanges.

Consider the ramifications of Schein's warning about telling people what they already know. How do you respond when treated in such a way? Reactions run the gamut from amusement to impatience to offense. The recipient almost always perceives him or herself as having been placed in an inferior position rather than one of equality and respect.

In a society whose organizations employ a high level of telling in interpersonal communication and problem solving, should it be a surprise that the level of engagement and respect between employees and leadership is so often low?

Our society tends to focus on what is broken. When the focus is only on the deficits, people become disempowered, discouraged, and demoralized. There can be little argument that many things remain broken in our society and workplaces, but the effective leader must find ways to shed light on a new direction with less negative potential than simply telling people only about the problems.

The Message of Asking

When one person asks a question of another, the person being asked is immediately empowered. Asking a question says, "I am making myself vulnerable to you." A certain amount of trust is implied. When a leader asks a question of another team member, the parties are placed on equal footing. The relationship becomes interdependent. When we engage in asking, the following statements are implied.

- I don't have complete knowledge of the situation.
- You have knowledge that may be important.
- I respect the fact that you are closer to the action and may have greater insight than me.
- I respect your ability to observe and analyze the situation.
- I am willing to listen to your thoughts and ideas.
- We are interdependent.

The practical experience and outcomes described in the writings of Captain Marquet, Captain Abrashoff, General McCrystal, and Dr. Schein all emphasize the importance of fully and completely embracing this mind-set in the pursuit of pinnacle performance.

Comparing the implied messages of asking and telling usually provokes reflection and discussion in workshops. There is probably no such thing as the right balance between asking and telling in the broad spectrum of leadership. It seems reasonable that any effort to improve one's leadership ability could rightly start with more asking and less telling.

In the book *Appreciative Inquiry in Healthcare*, the authors define appreciative inquiry (AI) as the study of what "gives life" to organizations, teams, and people when they are at their best. They suggest, and a large body of research supports the premise, that people learn and organizations change most readily when they focus on, study, and engage in dialogue about strengths, patterns of success, and who they are at their best.[4]

The practice of AI uses questions about what we value and appreciate to discover the best of who a team is. AI focuses on the shared vision to design a continually improving future. Like physicians, when effective leaders intervene in a situation, their purpose is always to help improve the situation and never to do harm.

Even with the best of intentions, we all have witnessed situations when leadership inflicted more harm than good. We are reminded of a Dilbert cartoon. In the last frame of the cartoon, Dilbert says, "Someday I hope to solve a problem that is not caused by leadership."

His boss quickly replies, "You'll never get that far!"[5]

The problems caused by leadership can most frequently be categorized as unintentional. Regardless of intention, they are problems, take time to solve, have real bottom-line costs, and cause considerable disengagement. We will never overcome all misunderstanding and miscommunication, but we can mitigate such problems by taking time before intervening to think through our approach. Asking the right questions at the right time can create a much smoother path for the future.

Asking the Right Question at the Right Time

Schein's research and experience offers some simple but very effective guidance on this issue. One of the problems leaders encounter in their many day-to-day encounters is getting to the unfiltered facts of a situation. Discovery of the real problem sometimes requires the skill of a mind reader and the patience of Mother Teresa.

People with a problem often don't know the source of the problem or, for various reasons, may not want to fully disclose all they know. In such situations, the leader runs into defensive mind-sets that build walls, which can be most difficult to get over.

The types of questions we ask and the sequence in which we ask them can create open dialogue and improve problem solving.

Schein suggests that questions can take different forms and help all participants uncover the real problems, motivations, and emotions. The first stage of questioning should be *pure inquiry*. Pure inquiry focuses only on what is going on. A few sample inquiries will clarify the point:

- Tell me what is going on.
- How can I help?
- Describe exactly what occurred.
- What happened next?
- When did this last happen?
- Can you describe the last time when this was not a problem and things were going well?
- Tell me more.[6]

Notice there is no judgment or presupposition about causality or blame. During this phase of inquiry, allow the participants to continue to talk until the discussion subsides of its own accord.

Toward the end, someone will likely offer a "what do you think?" question. *Be careful.* This can be a trap. Leaders too often fall into "instant expert" status. The trap springs because we may not have uncovered all the pertinent details; any solution offered will likely be little more than a Band-Aid.

The key point to look for when moving to the next phase of inquiry should be trust. Are the parties exhibiting any openness to increasing trust? Without an increase in trust, the likelihood of listening and open-minded reception remains low. Stay within the pure inquiry phase, using such questions as "What am I missing or not understanding about X?"

When the energy of pure inquiry subsides, it is time to enter *diagnostic inquiry.* The environment will shift from what occurred to the feelings and emotions that accompanied the occurrences described. The focus turns to those things that the participants probably chose not to report or explain initially.

If the leader had chosen to enter the picture at the outset, it would be much more likely that an environment of defensiveness would have arisen. Pure inquiry allows for the gathering of information without accusatory inference. It is built on the existing level of trust, or lack thereof. With that foundation, the leader can explore deeper into the realities of the situation. The stage is set to ask the how and why questions.

At this point, the leader is attempting to discover the feelings, motives, reactions, contemplated future actions, and potential reactions to contemplated actions. As Schein explains, the leader is working to help the participants learn and understand the complexities of what is and might occur within the overall system we experience as the workplace.[7]

Questions should start with the general and proceed to the specific as responses are probed. Some examples include the following:

- Why are you going in that direction?
- Have you tried other means of getting to that point in the past? What happened?

These questions lay the foundation and create a natural bridge to more difficult questions about feelings. Some examples include the following:

- How do you feel about that?
- What reactions did that arouse in you?
- What was your emotional reaction?

Cause and motive can now be explored with a simple shift of focus that will not set off inhibiting alarms within the participant group. Consider developing your set of questions from the following models:

- Why do you think we are having such a problem?
- Why do you think you reacted in such a manner?
- What do you think was the reason for the others' reaction?
- Have you seen or experienced such a reaction before?
- What was the reasoning behind your reaction?

Probing questions concerning responses to the above questions might enable the leader to delve more in-depth into actions taken or contemplated. For example:

- What did you do when that occurred?
- What was the response/outcome?
- What do you think is the best move from here?
- If you do X action, then how do you think Y person will react?

The last sample question makes an excellent probe that will enable you to move to the next phase.

By now, the reader is gaining understanding about getting deeper into the complexities involved in an organizational leadership situation. As we have discussed, the complexities of any system approach the infinite.

Before approaching a situation with your opinions and historically tested solutions, set the stage for greater reception. Based upon the foundational dialogue and understanding created by a planned set of progressively deeper questions, the leader becomes poised to present suggestions and establish an open dialogue for moving ahead, regardless of the severity of the starting point.

Schein described this last phase as *confrontational inquiry.*[8] Confrontational inquiry offers suggestions and ideas to the participants through questions, which invite openness and a sharing of ideas. It reflects shared leadership at its best: embracing the best thoughts from the diversity of experience and knowledge.

- Could we try X in an attempt to move forward?
- What are the possible outcomes if we try Z?
- How would other stakeholders react to such a move?

Questions can help a team move through their own conceptual and emotional landscape. With that as a foundation, the leader can introduce new ideas with the possibility of stronger buy-in and support.

At this stage, it is always good to check the temperature of the environment. The effective leader will want to know the following:

- How are we doing?
- Are we making progress?
- Are these questions helping to create understanding and potential paths for future success?

As always, the critical skill will be the ability of all parties, especially the leader, to listen and think about what is communicated.

Become a Consistently Effective Listener

As a leader, your ability to listen effectively is perhaps the most important of your communication skills. Yet many adults are in fact very poor listeners. There are numerous reasons for this, the most important one being that during our formative years, most of us receive little to no instruction in how to listen effectively.

Listening effectively is a learned skill that can be developed and improved. First, though, we must understand a few simple concepts about listening that affect our ability to be consistently effective listeners.

People most often communicate by voice, obviously creating sound that we hear. The key concept in listening effectively relates to the human abilities of receiving and processing sounds.

It important to make the distinction between hearing and listening. *Hearing* is our ability to perceive or take in sound through our physical hearing system. Assuming our hearing system is functioning properly, we take in all kinds of sounds on a constant basis.

Listening is what we do with sound. We give attention to, interpret, and attempt to grasp what is being conveyed to us. We listen to *create understanding* from the sounds we hear.

There are three factors of communication that impact our ability to listen effectively.

The typical adult can

- speak at about 150 words per minute,
- listen at about 500 words per minute, and
- think at about 1200 words per minute.

Consider carefully these three factors. A speaking rate of 150 words per minute is a large number of spoken words. The typical adult, with a listening capacity of about 500 words per minute, can handle this volume with ease if listening effectively. Listening capacity is over three times the speaking capacity of a typical adult. Our capacity to hear allows us to easily take in the words of even a fast talker.

At this point, an advantage is obvious. Our ability to listen to someone is much greater than their capacity to speak to us. Knowing this, it makes sense that listening effectively should be easy.

Unfortunately, it's not—because of our capacity to *think*. The thinking rate of a typical adult is about eight times faster than the same person's speaking rate, and more than twice as fast as the listening rate. In practical terms, this means that we think well ahead of the person speaking.

Most of us are predisposed to immediately respond without thinking about all of what's been said. This predisposition causes us to very often miss important details of what someone is saying to us. This predisposition creates miscommunication.

To become a consistently effective listener, the number one skill you must master is *learning to control your thinking speed*. This is not an easy thing to do. If you have ever attempted to finish a sentence for someone, then you just demonstrated the point. Your thinking speed was so far ahead of the other person's speaking speed that you thought you knew how to finish the comment, so you did. In the majority of such scenarios, one's completion of another's sentence is not even close to the speaker's intention. This failure to manage thinking speed causes us not to listen for understanding, but to listen for our opportunity to respond.

To become a consistently effective listener, listening must become a top-of-mind priority. This skill is not like that of learning to ride a bicycle—an easily repeatable skill that can be quickly recalled even if one has not been on a bicycle for many years. Being a consistently effective listener is not at all like this. It requires consistent attention to do it well.

This means the elimination of the ill-named concept known as *multitasking*. This means making eye contact when communicating, to help stay focused on what the person is saying. It means not blurting out a response. It means pausing a moment to think about how to respond. This is easy to say, but much harder to do for most people.

Becoming a consistently effective listener means putting down the mobile device or ignoring the keyboard and getting focused on the person speaking. It means not interrupting the person speaking until an appropriate point. Then it means asking questions to gain understanding, or make a confirming comment that lets the other person know that the message was understood. When we listen effectively and demonstrate that we are listening, we help to create meaningful dialogue and true understanding.

As a leader, your ability to be a consistently effective listener is another tool for building positive relationships. People sincerely appreciate it when they know their leader is listening and understanding whatever message is being conveyed.

Exercises for Reflection and Learning

1. Think about a recent circumstance at work when a significant miscommunication occurred. Note in writing all the details that you can recall. Examine the event, keeping in mind the ideas about communicating with others found throughout this chapter. Identify the root cause of the miscommunication, and then determine how the miscommunication could have been avoided.

2. Review the information in this chapter about being a consistently effective listener. Apply this information consciously throughout one day. At the end of the day, stop to reflect on what you experienced and learned. Did anyone react to you listening more intently? Did you on at least one occasion pause to think of your response to someone's question or comment before answering? Did you find that your actions helped to created more understanding for yourself and/or others?

11

FILLING THE RESERVOIR: A TRUE ACCOUNT OF REPLENISHING LEADERSHIP RESOURCES

There is a simpler way to organize human endeavor. It requires being in the world without fear. Being in the world with play and creativity. Seeking after what's possible. Being willing to learn and to be surprised.
–Margaret Wheatley and Myron Kellner-Rogers

For the last eleven years, we have dedicated ourselves to sharing the deeply held beliefs espoused in this book. We have been privileged to work with many people who showed the potential to become more effective and successful leaders.

In most cases, the only thing holding them back was the organizational culture in which they worked. "If it ain't broke, don't fix it" and "that's not the way we do it here" thinking hindered their efforts. We sincerely hope that our perspectives, ideas, advice, and practical how-tos have made you stop and consider how you and the other leaders/followers on your team can rise to a higher level of leadership. The leadership reservoir is low, and your untapped organizational talent is truly needed.

The ideas we have discussed are much more than theories. They are viable and can be implemented by those with the courage and desire to go to the next level of performance. To that end, we close with an actual case we were privileged to facilitate. The case description demonstrates how all the key concepts we have introduced can be incorporated in the real work environment.

The client was a large multistate, privately held, industrial company that decided to begin the process of growing their internal pool of high-potential talent. They wanted to begin by providing leadership training to their frontline supervisors, for the purpose of improving core leadership skills. They wanted a program design that would provide skills training and help identify supervisory leaders with potential for higher-level leadership.

After developing a program design that all agreed would meet the requirements, we began working with a group of twenty relatively short-tenured supervisors. Almost all had less than two years of supervisory experience, and they were drawn from various departments throughout the organization. They represented job functions from maintenance, accounting, sales, field services, and customer service. Most had only a high school education and had worked their way up from the entry level to their current positions.

The program ran for eight weeks. The group met on eight consecutive Monday evenings starting at six o'clock and running until around nine thirty. During this time, we covered virtually all the key leadership concepts discussed in this book, although packaged in their vernacular and context.

A crucial element of this training was to instill a confidence boost, showing we understood and appreciated the importance of their roles in the larger organization. Senior leadership wanted participants to recognize the company's interest in their futures, and the company's commitment to help each person prosper within the organization.

The customized training plan consisted of multiple approaches. Participants engaged in exercises designed to improve public speaking skills. These exercises helped increase individual confidence and allowed for spontaneous discussion of the importance of communication in leadership.

Participants came to realize the value of both delivery and listening in one-on-one and group communication. In such settings, participants could rapidly improve their communication and listening skills. It was quite amazing to see what people can accomplish in focused situations over an eight-week time frame.

Most notable was participants' increased ability to use conflict awareness and management as positive techniques for creativity and problem solving. The group, through work-related, interactive activities, became more cognizant of and comfortable with other key leadership topics, such as continuous improvement, delegation, building relationships, creating a vision, developing self-awareness, accountability, and responsibility.

Finally, and most importantly, each participant was charged with what we called an *application challenge*. All participants had to work with their direct reports and members of the group to identify one specific problem that existed in their respective areas. Each participant had to clearly identify the problem, examine all the causes of the problem, identify possible solutions to the problem and the necessary department interactions needed to enact each solution, and then implement the best solution. The "graduation" requirement tasked each participant to quantify, from a financial perspective, the impact of what he or she had decided to tackle, whether in cost reductions, labor cost savings, materials cost improvement, or whatever measures were applicable to the individual problem.

At the last session, the participants submitted written reports and presented the problems, how they went about addressing the problems, and the results achieved. Presentations were made to the group and three senior executives. As you might imagine, not all projects had reached a conclusion; some were works in progress. Regardless, participants were able to convey what they had learned and possible ways that knowledge and effort would directly benefit the company.

What an evening it turned out to be! By the time all the presentations were concluded, this group of twenty frontline, relatively inexperienced managers had implemented improvements with a direct bottom-line value in excess of $700,000. *Wow!*

The senior executives in attendance were lavish in their praise of this group and very excited about the results achieved. The participants were extremely proud of their results, both individually and collectively. They exuded pride and confidence. The executives were amazed at the creative thinking and solutions offered. Participants and senior leadership were mutually appreciative of the opportunity and the effort the program represented.

We offered the same program to another group from the same company just a few months later. Once again the people delivered sterling and unexpected results. We do not know what net financial benefit the company realized in this round. But again, participants exhibited increased confidence and offered actual cost-saving and performance improvements.

Unfortunately, 2007 ushered in a difficult business environment, and training and development budgets were cut. In an effort to increase efficiency and save money, this company postponed employee-development activities. Once again, mechanistic, top-down thinking was assumed to be the best wisdom for the time.

Who knows what a different mind-set of leader/follower continuum thinking might have been able to deliver? Recall the worst-to-first examples presented in previous chapters and ask the same question. Future outcomes are not and *never will be* mechanically predictable. Consider the potential of a simpler way. Give up some control. Have faith. Be prepared to be surprised.

Becoming an effective and successful leader/follower is a noble undertaking—and profitable! Yes, the change requires a new way of thinking, and it will not be easy. But it is fun, exciting, and inspiring.

And it works!

It is our wish that you will take all you have learned from what we have written, apply it, and discover your own pinnacle of success.

APPENDIX A

VROOM-YETTON MODEL

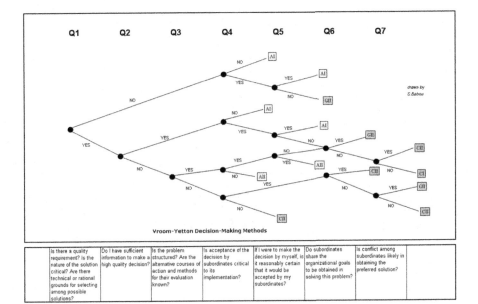

Q1	Q2	Q3	Q4	Q5	Q6	Q7	
Is there a quality requirement? Is the nature of the solution critical? Are there technical or rational grounds for selecting among possible solutions?	Do I have sufficient information to make a high quality decision?	Is the problem structured? Are the alternative courses of action and methods for their evaluation known?	Is acceptance of the decision by subordinates critical to its implementation?	If I were to make the decision by myself, is it reasonably certain that it would be accepted by my subordinates?	Do subordinates share the organizational goals to be obtained in solving this problem?	Is conflict among subordinates likely in obtaining the preferred solution?	

APPENDIX B

DISC CHARACTERISTICS

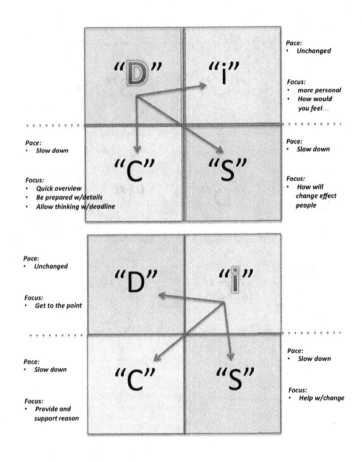

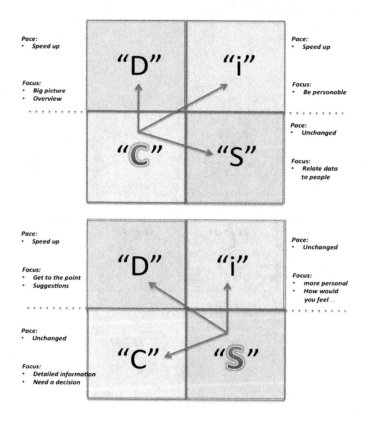

Pace:
- Speed up

Focus:
- Big picture
- Overview

"D" "i" "C" "S"

Pace:
- Speed up

Focus:
- Be personable

Pace:
- Unchanged

Focus:
- Relate data to people

Pace:
- Speed up

Focus:
- Get to the point
- Suggestions

"D" "i" "C" "S"

Pace:
- Unchanged

Focus:
- more personal
- How would you feel…

Pace:
- Unchanged

Focus:
- Detailed information
- Need a decision

APPENDIX C

GAPS COACHING

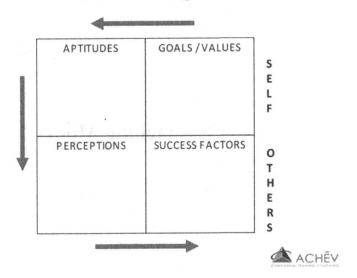

GAPS Coaching Model

APTITUDES	GOALS / VALUES
PERCEPTIONS	SUCCESS FACTORS

SELF

OTHERS

ACHĒV

GAPS Coaching Model

APTITUDES	GOALS / VALUES
PERCEPTIONS	SUCCESS FACTORS

S E L F

O T H E R S

What are your Goals and Values?

❖ Are they congruent with the company's goals and values?

❖ Do any conflicts exist?

❖ Are they realistic and attainable?

❖ Are you dedicated to achieving them?

GAPS Coaching Model

APTITUDES	GOALS / VALUES
PERCEPTIONS	SUCCESS FACTORS

S E L F

O T H E R S

What Aptitudes (skills and knowledge) are needed to achieve your goals?

❖ Which do you currently have?

❖ What's needed?

❖ What are your thoughts on development?

GAPS Coaching Model

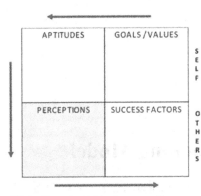

APTITUDES	GOALS / VALUES
PERCEPTIONS	SUCCESS FACTORS

*Note: If the coaching session strictly involves a measurable set of skills, it may be advisable to skip the perceptions discussion.

What are the Perceptions* of those who work with you?

Note the change in orientation from a self-evaluation to discussing the perceptions of others

❖ What is the foundation for your conviction?

❖ Would others agree with your assessment?

❖ Who would not? Why?

❖ May I share my thoughts and observations with you?

 ACHĒV

GAPS Coaching - Perceptions

Be ready for some common reactions:

"They don't understand me"
"That's not correct"
"That's not what I mean"
"They're not being truthful"
"That's not the real me"

All may be true, but....

IT DOESN'T MATTER!!!

 ACHĒV

GAPS Coaching Model

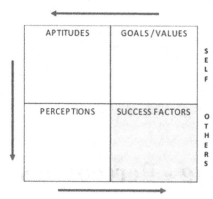

What are the **Success Factors** that
must take place to reach your goals?

❖ What skills and knowledge must
   be acquired?

❖ Do any perceptions need to change?

❖ What is the action plan?

❖ What support is available?

❖How will success/progress be
   measured?

APPENDIX D

DETERMINING YOUR PERSONAL VALUES

Recognition	Competence	Commitment
Family	Money / Wealth	Effectiveness
Responsible	Honesty	Customer satisfaction
Loyalty	Faith / Religion	Accept Change
Teamwork	Legacy	Fairness
Life Balance	Benevolence	Knowledge
Tolerance	Authority	Status
Integrity	Quality	Growth
Creativity / Innovation	Compassion	Perfection
Trust	Achievement	Independence
Independence	Accountability	Courage
Passion	Fitness	Diligence

List your top ten core personal values. Next, reduce that list to your top six values. Then narrow your list to your top three values. Feel free to list any personal value that you desire, including ones not shown above.

Top Ten Values	Top Six Values	Top Three Values
_____	_____	_____
_____	_____	_____
_____	_____	_____
_____	_____	
_____	_____	
_____	_____	
_____		
_____		
_____		
_____		

Personal Alignment: Your Values/Action Rating (VAR)

Directions: First, write down in the space provided below your top three core personal values from the previous exercise. Then rate the degree to which you act in accordance with those values, using the scale below.

1 = I always act 100 percent in accordance with this value.

2 = I often act in accordance with this value (about 75 percent of the time).

3 = I act in accordance with this value about half the time.

4 = I act in accordance with this value about a quarter of the time.

5 = I act in accordance with this value less than 25 percent of the time.

Personal Core Value	Your Rating

Personal alignment addresses the fundamental question, to what extent do you act in accordance with your values? Alignment applies to work and nonwork life. It focuses on such issues as the extent to which you:

- Allocate your time in accordance with your values—at work? At home?
- Consistently treat other people the way you want to—at work? At home?
- Do the things you want to do that reflect your values.

The more you live and work in accordance with your values, the more you feel whole. The alternative, constantly sacrificing your values, leads to feeling f-r-a-g-m-e-n-t-e-d. When you are fragmented, you do not feel like you are doing what you are meant to do, and your energy and motivation are easily depleted.

REFERENCES

Introduction

1. Heifetz, Ronald A. (1994). *Leadership without easy answers.* Boston, MA: Harvard.
2. Charan, Ram (2008). *Leaders at all levels.* San Francisco, CA: Wiley.
3. Marquet, L. David (2012). *Turn the ship around.* New York, NY: Penguin.
4. Kouzes, J. K., & Posner, B. Z. (2016). *Learning leadership.* San Francisco, CA: Wiley.
5. Kellerman, Barbara (2012). *The end of leadership.* New York, NY: HarperCollins.
6. Dweck, Carol (2006). *Mindset.* New York, NY: Ballantine.

Chapter 1

1. Gladwell, Malcolm. (2002, July 22). The talent myth. *New Yorker.*
2. Taylor, Frederick W. (1911). *The principles of scientific management.* New York, NY: Harper & Brothers.
3. Merrill, Douglas C., & Martin, James A. (2011). *Getting organized in the Google era.* New York, NY: Crown Publishing.
4. Hough, J., & White, M. (2009). Once upon a time there was an organization: Organizational stories as antithesis to fairy tales. *Journal of Management Inquiry*, 15–25.
5. Bass, Bernard (2008). *The Bass handbook of leadership.* New York, NY: Free Press.

6. Wrege, C., & Perroni, A. (1974). Taylor's pig tale: A historical analysis of Frederick W. Taylor's pig-iron experiments. *Academy of Management Journal, 17,* 6–27.

7. Kanigel, Robert (1997). *The one best way: Frederick W. Taylor and the enigma of efficiency.* New York, NY: Viking.

8. Plenkiewicz, Peter (2010). *The executive guide to business process management: How to maximize lean and Six Sigma and see your bottom line explode.* Bloomington, IN: iUniverse.

9. Kellerman, Barbara (2012). *The end of leadership.* New York, NY: HarperCollins.

10. Boyatzis, R.,. & Case, A. R. (1989). The impact of an MBA program on managerial ability. *Journal of Management Development, 8*(5), 66–77.

11. Kellerman, Barbara (2012). *The end of leadership.* New York, NY: HarperCollins.

12. Gladwell, Malcolm (2002, July 22). The talent myth. *New Yorker.*

13. Dweck, Carol (2006). *Mindset.* New York, NY: Ballantine.

14. Ibid.

15. Choi, T., Dooley, K., & Rungtusanatham, M. (2001). Supply networks and complex adaptive systems: Control versus emergence. *Journal of Operations Management, 19,* 351–366.

Chapter 2

1. Drucker, Peter (1998, October 5). Management's new paradigm. *Forbes.*

2. Marion, Russ (1999). *The edge of organization.* Thousand Oaks, CA: SAGE Publications.

3. Liker, Jeffrey (2004). *The Toyota way.* New York, NY: McGraw-Hill.

4. Ibid.

5. Womack, J., & Jones, D. (1996). *Lean Thinking.* New York: Free Press.

6. Marquet, L. David (2012). *Turn the ship around.* New York, NY: Penguin.

7. Ibid.

8. Choi, T., Dooley, K., & Rungtusanatham, M. (2001). Supply networks and complex adaptive systems: Control versus emergence. *Journal of Operations Management, 19*, 351–366

9. Kellerman, Barbara (2012). *The end of leadership*. New York, NY: HarperCollins.

10. Abrashoff, D. M. (2008). *It's our ship*. New York, NY: Business Plus.

Chapter 3

Epigraph: Tjan, A. K., Harrington, R. J., & Hsieh, T. Y. (2012). *Heart, smarts, guts, and luck: What it takes to be an entrepreneur and build a great business*. Boston, MA: HBS.

1. Gardner, Howard (1997). *Extraordinary minds*. New York, NY: Basic Books.

2. Dweck, Carol (2006). *Mindset*. New York, NY: Ballantine.

3. Ibid.

4. Ibid.

5. Quigley, Michael (2002). Leaders as learners. *Executive Excellence, 19*(9).

6. Zigarmi, D., Fowler, S., & Lyles, D. (2007). *Achieve leadership genius*. Upper Saddle River, NJ: FT Press.

7. Shakespeare, William. *Hamlet*, ed. (Barnes and Noble, 1994), act 1, scene 3, line 78.

8. Zigarmi, D., Fowler, S., & Lyles, D. (2007). *Achieve leadership genius*. Upper Saddle River, NJ: FT Press.

9. Wiley & Sons. *Everything DiSC by Inscape Publications*. Hoboken, NJ.

Chapter 4

1. Brauns, Chris (2010, June). "Where there is no vision, the people perish": One of the most misapplied verses in the Bible. *A Brick In the Valley*. Retrieved from http://chrisbrauns.com/2010/06/where-there-is-no-vision-the-people-perish-one-of-the-mostmisinterpreted-verses-in-the-bible/.

2. De Chardin, Pierre T. (2004). *The future of man.* New York, NY: Penguin.
3. Nanus, Burt (1992). *Visionary leadership.* San Francisco, CA: Jossey-Bass.
4. Peale, Norman V. (1988). *Power of the plus factor.* New York, NY: Fawcett.
5. Jing, F., Avery, G., & Bergensteiner, H. (2014). Enhancing performance in small professional firms through vision communication and sharing. *Asia Pacific Journal of Management, 31*(2).
6. Welch, Jack (2005). *Winning.* New York, NY: HarperCollins.
7. Kotter, John P. (1996). *Leading change.* Boston, MA: Harvard Business School Press.
8. Ibid.
9. Snyder, N. H., Dowd, J. J., & Houghton, D. M. (1994). *Vision, values, and courage.* New York, NY: The Free Press.
10. Maxwell, John (2014). *Good leaders ask great questions.* New York, NY: Center Street.
11. Nanus, Burt (1992). *Visionary leadership.* San Francisco, CA: Jossey-Bass.
12. Ibid.
13. Ibid.
14. Grant, Adam (2012). Leading with meaning: Beneficiary contact, prosocial impact, and the performance effects of transformational leadership. *Academy of Management Journal. 55*(2), 456–476.

Chapter 5

1. Katzenbach, Jon R., & Smith, Douglas K. (1993). *The wisdom of teams.* Boston, MA: Harvard Business School Press.
2. McChrystal, Stanley (2015). *Team of teams.* New York, NY: Penguin.
3. Liker, Jeffrey (2014). *Developing lean leaders at all levels.* Lean Leadership Institute.
4. Wooden, John (2005). *Wooden on leadership.* New York, NY: McGraw-Hill.

5. Willink, Jocko, & Babin, Leif (2015). *Extreme ownership.* New York, NY: St. Martin's Press.

6. McChrystal, Stanley (2015). *Team of teams.* New York, NY: Penguin.

7. Ibid.

8. Ibid.

9. Ibid.

10. Welch, Jack (2005). *Winning.* New York, NY: HarperCollins.

11. Ibid.

12. Pentland, Alex (2012). The new science of building great teams. *Harvard Business Review.*

13. Ibid.

14. Ibid.

Chapter 6

1. Van Vugt, Mark, & Ahuja, Anjana (2011). *Naturally selected: The evolutionary science of leadership.* New York, NY: Harper Business.

2. Kellerman, Barbara (2012). *Followership.* New York, NY: HarperCollins.

3. Pentland, Alex (2012). The new science of building great teams. *Harvard Business Review.*

4. Maxwell, John (1998). *The 21 irrefutable laws of leadership.* Nashville, TN: Thomas Nelson.

5. Senge, Peter (1990). *The fifth discipline.* New York, NY: Doubleday.

6. Wooden, John (2005). *Wooden on leadership.* New York, NY: McGraw-Hill.

7. Hough, J., & White, M. (2009). Once upon a time there was an organization: Organizational stories as antithesis to fairy tales. *Journal of Management Inquiry,* 15–25.

8. Weber, Linda, & Carter, Allison (2003). *The social construction of trust.* New York, NY: Kluwer Academic/Plenum.

9. Fleming, John (2007). *Human sigma.* New York, NY: Gallup Press.

10. Selby, John (2007). *Listening with empathy.* Charlottesville, VA: Hampton Roads.

11. King, Martin Luther (1963). *Letter from Birmingham jail.* New York, NY: HarperCollins.
12. Cooper, Robert (2001). *The other 90%.* New York, NY: Crown Business.
13. Welch, Jack (2005). *Winning.* New York, NY: HarperCollins.

Chapter 7

1. Wooden, John (2005). *Wooden on leadership.* New York, NY: McGraw-Hill.
2. Senge, Peter (1990). *The fifth discipline.* New York, NY: Doubleday.
3. Bushe, G., & Marshak, R. (2016). The dialogic mindset: Leading emergent change in a complex world. *34*(1), 37–6
4. Senge, Peter (1990). *The fifth discipline.* New York, NY: Doubleday.
5. Bicking, Cortes (2015). *Toyota production system(TPS) theories-in-action and lean theories-in-action: A contrast in maximization of human potential* (Doctoral dissertation). Available from ProQuest-CSA.
6. Senge, Peter (1990). *The fifth discipline.* New York, NY: Doubleday.
7. Ibid.
8. Ibid.
9. Izumi-Taylor, S., Wang, L. Weiping, & Ogawa, Tetsuya (2005). I think, therefore I improve: A qualitative study of concepts of hansei (introspection) among Japanese adults. *Journal of Early Childhood Teacher.*
10. Senge, Peter (1990). *The fifth discipline.* New York, NY: Doubleday.
11. Schon, Donald (1983). *The reflective practitioner.* New York, NY: Basic Books.
12. Ibid.
13. Liker, Jeffrey (2004). *The Toyota way.* New York, NY: McGraw-Hill.
14. Izumi-Taylor, S., Wang, L. Weiping, & Ogawa, Tetsuya (2005). I think, therefore I improve: A qualitative study of concepts of hansei (introspection) among Japanese adults. *Journal of Early Childhood Teacher.*
15. Wooden, John (2005). *Wooden on leadership.* New York, NY: McGraw-Hill.

Chapter 9

1. Sousa, David A. (2012). *Brainwork*. Bloomington, IN: Triple Nickel Press.
2. DeMuth, Christopher (2017, February 11–12). The method in Trump's tumult. *Wall Street Journal*, p. A11.
3. Ibid.
4. Dana, Daniel (2001). *Conflict resolution*. New York, NY: McGraw-Hill.
5. Sousa, David A. (2012). *Brainwork*. Bloomington, IN: Triple Nickel Press.
6. Dana, Daniel (2001). *Conflict resolution*. New York, NY: McGraw-Hill.

Chapter 10

1. Schein, Edgar (2013). Humble inquiry. San Francisco, CA: Berrett-Koehler.
2. Schein, Edgar (2011). *Helping*. San Francisco, CA: Berrett-Koehler.
3. Schein, Edgar (2013). *Humble inquiry*. San Francisco, CA: Berrett-Koehler.
4. May, N., Becker, D., Frankel. R., Haizlip, J., Harmon, R., Plews-Ogan, M., Schorling, J., Williams, A., & Whitney, D. (2011). *Appreciative inquiry in healthcare*. Brunswick, OH: Custom Publishing.
5. Scott Adams – http://www.dilbert.com – United Feature Snydicate, Inc., Date Unknown
6. Schein, Edgar (2013). *Humble inquiry*. San Francisco, CA: Berrett-Koehler.
7. Ibid.
8. Ibid.

INDEX

G

Gallup organization, 62
GAPS coaching model, 115–118
Gardner, Howard, 23
Gladwell, Malcolm, 1, 4
Goldsmith, Marshall, 1
Good Leaders Ask Great Questions
    (Maxwell), 37
Grant, Adam, 41
"the great man" theory, 9
growth mindset, 5

H

hansei, 69, 72
Harrington, R., 23
Harvard University, 3
hearing, as distinguished from
    listening, 104
Heifetz, Ronald, xiii–xiv, xv
Helping (Schein), 95
hiring, through vision, 41
holistic perspectives/thinking, 11
hoshin kanri, 46
hospital administration, field of, 15
how and why, benefit of/need for, 10
Hsieh, T., 23
humble inquiry, 95
Humble Inquiry (Schein), 95

I

incremental change, four stages of, 1–2
"Information Filters," 25*f*
interconnectedness, 12
interpersonal conflict, 87
introversion, 30
It's Our Ship (Abrashoff), 16

J

Japanese culture, 46, 69, 72
Jing, F., 34

Journal of Operations Management, 6
journaling, 73–74
Jung, Carl, 28

K

kaizen, 72
Katzenbach, Jon, 45
Kellerman, Barbara, xv, 4, 18, 53
Kellner-Rogers, Myron, 107
King, Martin Luther, Jr., 62–63
Kotter, John, 36–37
Kouzes, James, xiv, xv

L

"the Law of the Lid," 55, 56
leader/follower concept, 53–54
leader/follower continuum, 18
leader/follower contract, 54–55
leaders, as learners, 23
Leaders at All Levels (Charan), xiv
leadership
    as 24-7 job, x
    bottom-up leadership, 11
    character of, vii
    characteristics and skills of, xi
    command-and-control leadership
        methods, 9–10
    as communication process, 26
    measuring leadership success,
        46–47
    principles of. *See* principles of
        leadership
    replenishing resources for, 107–110
    thinking as first step and
        prerequisite action for, 27
    as viewed from multiplicative
        perspective rather than
        additive one, 47
leadership drought
    evidence of, 7
    evolution of, 1–7

Printed in the United States
By Bookmasters